praise for *trans-forming proclamation*

"I'm endlessly curious about and fascinated with the spiritual paths and practices of my trans family. Where do we go for refuge when we're in the grip of overwhelming gender-based desires, anger, and confusion? *Trans-forming Proclamation: A Transgender Theology of Daring Existence* is a path of joyful, queer, Judaic mysticism, and ecosexuality; at once ecstatic and academic, challenging and comforting. It's Talmudic wisdom for the rest of us. Thank you, Liam M. Hooper, old friend, for this soul-nourishing vision of gender, trans and beyond."

~ Kate Bornstein, author of
Gender Outlaw: On Men, Women and the Rest of Us

"*Trans-Forming Proclamation: A Transgender Theology of Daring Existence* is the most comprehensive constructive trans theology I've ever read. Indeed, this is the book I wished I had when I was a closeted theology professor afraid to come out as trans! Drawing out rich connections between his grandmother's Scottish-Muskogee Indigenous wisdom and our shared Jewish ancestors, Liam M. Hooper proclaims not only a message but a method that is original and liberating. This comprehensive and scholarly, yet practical and personally engaging book is highly recommended for scholars interested in religious studies, gender studies, and queer studies."

~ The Rev. Dr. Donovan Ackley III, Current Adjunct Professor at University of Redlands; former Chair of the Department of Theology and Philosophy at Azusa Pacific University.

"In language bursting with vitality, theologian Liam M. Hooper exhorts transgender people to recognize their lives as "living proclamations." Rejecting a view of the world as it has been narrowly constructed in favor of one which sees the world teeming with diversity as it actually is, Hooper's book of vital insights is a great gift, not only to transgender people but to us all."

~ Rabbi Mark Sameth, author of *The Name: A History of the Dual-Gendered Hebrew Name for God*.

"Liam M. Hooper tenderly explores gender and the Bible in a work that defies genre. With rich patches of poetry, memoir, and devotional, Hooper weaves together his inspiring literary insights with grounded, original, and informed scholarship. *Trans-Forming Proclamation: A Transgender Theology of Daring Existence* is new wine in a new wine skin. Inventive, artful, and liberating."

~ Peterson Toscano, performance activist and Bible scholar, creator of *Transfigurations—Transgressing Gender in the Bible*

"We have had centuries of imposed dead-ends, shameful disenfranchisement, and warped consanguinity on our roads to the Divine energy. This book shines a light on a soft, tender path that can lead anyone—but especially gender nonconforming folks—to that same energy we have been told was not our birthright. This book is an invitation to step into and find solace in that Divine embrace that is yours just as much as it is anyone else's."

~ Diamond Stylz, executive director of Black Trans Women, Inc and producer of *Marsha's Plate* podcast

"*Trans-forming Proclamation* goes beyond theology to offer us a political framework for navigating the world while reminding us that the rituals and tools transgender people create to survive are actually gifts to the world. Liam M. Hooper invites us to move forward in a way that honors and acknowledges all of humanity while taking care of the most vulnerable among us."

~ Enzi Tanner, healing-centered coach

"An amazing, wonderful, and much needed book. If you accept Liam M. Hooper's invitation into the Sacred Grove, you may not want to return. But as you read on, he shows us how our Groves—sacred sources of our existence, resilience, and resistance—are with and within us, always, wherever we go."

~ Mycroft Masada, nonbinary Jewish trans leader

"This rich book speaks powerfully to the divine creative imagination, in all its diverse and diffuse beauty, as found in the lives and experiences of trans and gender-expansive people. Trans identity is shown to be an authentic, positive reflection of the image of God in humans, who are understood here as existing alongside and being able to learn from the whole breadth of creation. Liam M. Hooper offers the possibility of a life-giving place for trans people in an often ill-fitting, inhospitable world, and claims trans people's right to seek after the God who, in Hooper's own words, 'abides with and speaks to us.'"

~ Susannah Cornwall,
Associate Professor of Constructive Theologies,
University of Exeter, UK

"Glory hallelujah! Liam M. Hoopers's Trans-forming Proclamation: A Transgender Theology of Daring Existence is a thought-provoking must-read selection. Each chapter is carefully crafted with passion, honesty, and a great deal of love. Liam's rich use of scripture will open the mind of any-one who truly wants to find the truth of transgender, intersex, and gender non-conforming persons. He carefully mines his own lived experience with bold conviction to provide a wealth of information about those of us most of the world has yet to understand. The poetic beauty and wise insights jump off the page to give the reader a remarkable understanding of "gen-der-transcendent" people. It is such a strong, engaging, and sophisticated piece of writing that I had a hard time putting it down. Well done!"

~ Rev. Debra Hopkins
Executive Director, There's Still Hope
Author of *Not Until You Have Walked In My Shoes:
A Journey of Discovery & The Spirit of the Human Heart*

trans-forming proclamation

trans-forming proclamation

A

Transgender

Theology

of

Daring

Existence

liam m. hooper

OtherWise Engaged Publishing

First edition December 2020
Cover and text design by Diana Coe / Crone Communications
Cover art by Liam M. Hooper
Author photograph by Shawn Hooper / Highland
Creations Photography

ISBN: 978-1-951124-23-6 (Paperback)
ISBN: 978-1-951124-24-3 (Hardcover)
ISBN: 978-1-951124-25-0 (Kindle Edition)
eISBN: 978-1-951124-26-7

Published by OtherWise Engaged Publishing
http://www.otherwiseengaged4u.wordpress.com

For the kindred who have gone before, especially:
Virginia Ramey Mollenkott, Monica Roberts,
Minister Bobbie Jean Baker, and Leslie Feinberg;
for Grandma Daught, Grandpa Mac,
Barb, Woody, and Dave.

For all of us who remain—
we, the still living, still proclaiming.

And for Diana.

# contents

preface ix

to tell you everything xv

introduction xvii

chapter one   Daring Existence 1

chapter two   Words Matter 9

chapter three   Our Stories about God 17

chapter four   Sacred Grove, Living Proclamation 25

chapter five   Holy Imaginaries —

                   Incomprehensible and Interconnected 37

                   ≈   Proclamations of Troubling Imagination 38

                   ≈   Expressing God's Image 40

                   ≈   Enspirited, Spiritual Beings 42

                   ≈   Creating Relationship 44

                   ≈   Divine Surgery 46

                   ≈   Authenticity in Relationship 50

                   ≈   Breaking Open the Binary 52

                   ≈   Holy Imaginaries, Divine Imagination 56

chapter six   Shedding Skin 61

chapter seven   Holy Set-Apartness 69

chapter eight   Beyond the Gates of the City 79

chapter nine   Taking Our Place in the Divine Imaginary 93

chapter ten   Completing the Circle: Returning to the

Grove 105

chapter eleven   Trans-forming Proclamation 113

≈   What Is Proclamation? 117

≈   Christian Preaching vs. Prophetic Proclamation 119

≈   What Is Trans-Forming? 123

≈   What Are the Assumptions of Trans-Forming

Proclamation? 128

≈   Practicing Trans-Forming Proclamation 134

epilogue   Unmistakable Sounds 141

resources for the journey 143

acknowledgments 149

about the author 153

preface

Given the topics underlying this work, it seems important to acknowledge some things about who I am. My perspectives as a gender theorist, theological activist, trans advocate, educator, and writer are shaped by my own experience and dispositions. None of us grows or lives in a vacuum, nor arises independently. Professionally, I benefited from a fair amount of education (through scholarships and student loans)—though I generally think that degrees are not all they are made out to be, I am grateful for what I learned in undergraduate and graduate studies. I received training in biological psychology and critical, social, and systems theory, during dual studies in psychology and literature, as well as practical training and credentialing in addictions counseling for several years following. Later, I received a Master of Divinity in which I focused on theological interpretation, clinical pastoral education, and spiritual formation.

Gleanings of my own trans journey are revealed in this work and inform my late-blooming transition. I turned forty-nine years of age about two weeks before my first shot of testosterone. That same week, I began the equally transformative seminary studies that, ultimately, began my journey to Judaism. Initially, while in college, I worked as a theater technician and production assistant, then became an HIV/AIDS case manager during the height of the AIDS crisis. Following that, for over twenty years, I was an addictions counselor and clinical director, specializing in co-occuring conditions and crisis stabilization, as well as LGBTQ-specific concerns impacting mental health and appropriate person-centered care. Throughout my life, I have volunteered with various AIDS service organizations, LGBTQ service groups, and, specifically, with trans advocacy groups. In hard times, I have also worked as an electrician's helper, construction worker, and landscaper. All these experiences, all the contemplations and reflections during, and since, significantly influence my work and who I am.

Thus, like any of us, I write from my own experience, formation, and location, as well as my own curiosities, investigations, ongoing learning, and theoretical dispositions. But there is far too much to say about all that. So, I will simply acknowledge I come to this work as a white, male-blending transgender person of complicated European and Indigenous descent, raised in the constructs of Christendom. That is, I am equally, and messily, enculturated in whiteness and white-blending. I descend, maternally, from Scottish highlanders and Muscogee Indians, who formed me, and from Hungarian immigrants I never met on my biological father's side. My formation embodies all the tensions, missteps, lessons, moments of good process, mistakes, and culturally-transmitted life-ways passed on to me. I bear, too, the experiences of having moved back and forth between the North and the South, and settling, again, back in the south.

I carry within me—in my very skin—all the tensions, potential insights, troubling and equally hopeful implications, contradictions, and possibilities for greater meaning infused in my lineage and formative experiences. I endeavor to work through, and with, the call to be mindful of, and engage ways of learning from, all these formative forces. This, to be sure, has been and is a life-long process. All of it, thus far, makes for a larger story for another time. Yet, the influences of that continuing internal work scatter throughout these pages. It is my hope those small offerings, as they appear, are helpful to the work of this project—more, I hope they will help you, my kindred, come to know me a little in positive and relatable ways.

In terms of scholarly theory and theology, I connect strongly with Jewish and process theologies. I have a respectful affinity for feminist semiotics, Black, lesbian, Marxist-feminist, and Womanist writers who have influenced me greatly—sometimes even in the negative, as with the racist and transphobic feminists. I have been profoundly influenced by liberation theologians from Gustavo Gutiérrez to James H. Cone, M. Shawn Copeland, and the liberative, practical mysticism of Howard Thurman. As well, I am influenced by a host of anti-racism, white supremacy-naming, patriarchy-debunking, decolonizing thinkers from bell hooks to Mab Segrest, Audre Lorde to Tema Okun, from James Baldwin to Winona LaDuke, Ta-Nehisi Coates and Ibram X. Kendi, more recently. I have also been shaped and formed by decades of queer theory and queer theology, including Leslie Feinberg, Riki Wilchins, Kate Bornstein, and Joy Ladin. Most notably, Jewish theology from all branches, as well as secular movements like Alcoholics Anonymous, and the study of systems theory and psychology have influenced me much more than dominant-culture Christian theologians. The list is too long to encapsulate and grows as I do. Still, the ideas and proclamations, here, are my own, born of my own experience, study, meditation, reflection, observation, thoughtful consideration, and interpretative blending of disciplines.

I come to these pages gratefully aware that my place here was forged by the creative resilience, contributions, joys, sorrows, tears, blood, and wisdom of those fearless trans ancestor-warriors, rabble-rousers, artists, writers, and life-way-makers who came before me (May their memories be blessings). None of us survives, or thrives, alone. On the gravel road to and from the Grove, where sometimes deer come walking, I continue to be sustained and shaped by a wide and diverse gathering of fellow seeker-travelers; they also walk with me. I come bearing, too and tenderly, anticipation of those of you already among us, finding your voice. This book is an out-reaching expression of love for them, those of us who are here—we, the still-living—and those who come after us. In the end, this book is a thing I long to tell, infused with stories, freedom-dreaming visions, and hidden artifacts I wish someone had shared with me, long before I began to understand them for myself.

My own journey toward developing this theory about human personhood began at an early age. That is, it began when I began to talk about being a boy and continued to unfold in my process through the experiences, consequences, and self-seeking discovery that followed. The era into which I was born was even less friendly to gender-transcendent persons than our current gender-troubled times. It seems that, even at the young age of six or so, I believed that people—including me—were capable of knowing, internally, who they are.

That is, I assumed that a person could sense who they are—even who they might be—then make self-actualizing choices based upon such self-knowledge. Apparently, the psychiatrists my parents reached out to for help disagreed with me.

They medicated me. The medication flattened and subdued me, altered my personality. It made me more docile and compliant, which in turn, made the rest of my treatment more successful. There was, indeed, more treatment. My psychiatrists advised me that I was a girl, I would always be a girl, and I needed to accept that and be happy with my life. These were powerful messages, aided by medication, that taught me other lessons as well. Lessons it has taken decades of striving intention and practice to recover from: do not talk about myself to others; be wary of people who claim to be helping me; saying certain things gets me in trouble; do not trust others without very good cause; and, paradoxically and more damning, it is likely I cannot trust myself either.

Those troubling messages compounded the fundamental lessons. I learned that something was wrong with me. I came to understand that I simply was not quite right. I lived with the implication that I would never, really, be grown—more, I might never know who I am. I would, it seemed, always be surrounded by those who were older, smarter, and more capable than me of knowing who I am. My instincts, my knowledge, my sense of things could never really be trusted. I learned I was incompetent, flawed somehow, and that I had, somehow, in some unknown way, chosen to be flawed. And yet, something in me did not quite believe all this. Something in me rebelled, in a quiet, dulled, and persistent selfhood-grasping way. Although all of this was bad enough, the medication had other long-lasting, troubling effects.

The medication they introduced into my sensitive, still-forming brain affected the systems that form, store, mark, and retrieve memories. Most of my memories from my formative years are a rather ethereal, faint, and tangled bundle of emotional sensations, partial images, and vague, shapeless forms of internal knowing that seem to float near, but never really reach, a solid grounding surface. Even now, I struggle to keep all but the most significant of memories for extended periods of time. The medication also chemically dissociated me. But, the brain learns from such treatment. Even when the medication was removed, the dissociative tendencies remained. In a foggy, shadowy mist of strangely self-integrated yet estranged connectedness, I learned, unconsciously, to function, move through the world with others, and discern remnant pieces of wounded personhood. Additionally, for me, temporal time is the fact of the ocean: real and fluid, yet oddly vaporous, like fog riding wave after repetitive wave of the same rolling sea. Through the commingling forces of will, intuition, and instinct, I learned to be and become a person.

I survived because of a single, profoundly life-saving human truth—one fundamentally relevant to a Trans-Forming Proclamation: the body knows, always, what a tender mind struggles to comprehend and process. A body remembers who a body is. There are always signals: sensations of dissonance and consonance, flickerings of light-filled insights, perceptions of body-brain memories. The self remains. The self survives. In spite of everything that seeks to submerge, subjugate, or destroy the endowed, indwelling sense of selfhood, selfhood rises. Selfhood persists. Selfhood asserts personhood. And, personhood proclaims. I am, like all of us, a living, evolving product of my continued living-on—in these particular times and circumstances. My experiences shape how I bear witness to, observe, accompany, reflect on, and interpret the experiences of others in my life.

My thoughts and theories about selfhood are shaped by all this, as well as my training, my experiences in recovering communities, and by the gifts of my own and others' living on. I say this to say that this work is also shaped by my continual experience of the Something More beyond me, yet with me, known and unknowable, which ever abides and sustains. It is my hope there is something, here, in my expressions of ideas, possibilities, and dreams of freedom that resonates with others.

May we continue to find and share with one another all manner of revelations, transcendent and mundane, in our collective searching for some Holy Presence amid the scatterings of dreams—lived, written, and living, still—left for us to excavate, ponder, interpret, and perhaps find in them some means for our communal thriving, spiritual vitality, and liberation.

May we come and go together, carrying sacred texts in paper and within our own skin, from the grove where deer and even fire-flies emerge, to speak and listen, sharing truths we find at kitchen tables, outdoor cafes, backyard circles, at podiums, pulpits, and plac-es in between. May we continue creating, together, communities of truth-seeking and relational discovery in the living of our miracu-lous, ever-proclaiming lives.

to tell you everything

I want to tell you
of the night I walked after dusk
with the deer. I want to tell you
so that you might see it; I want, really, to tell
you everything that feels needful, but will start

with this: that the tree leaves, turned
outward in wait of coming rain,
shimmered silver in the fading light:
before a rain, deer will run, feed, find shelter.
In the forest, at the gravel road's edge—
glimmering flashes of stark-still eyes, shining
in the canopy-sprays of rising moonlight falling: above,
here, there, and over there as well:
star-light pins pierced the woodland scrim of sky.

I stood, silent, receiving; their presence, an offering;
the empty road, a welcome stillness. In time,
the buck stepped out of the dark, points proudly
forward, so near I could have touched him. The doe
followed, slowed, and pausing, like this, turned her head
my way—an invitation, perhaps, to walk softly just behind
as she led her fawns into the cover of the woods, and glanced
back, only a moment; then, quietly, moving farther
into the trees, they left me alone

in the grace of their passing. This,
this telling, is for you—a thing I long
to show you; my response to something
the world, alive, tells us endlessly:
that God comes to us
everywhere.

introduction

 I want, really, to tell you everything needful; that is, I want to speak of things that seem somehow important to say about this idea of living proclamation; and, too, about standing in the Grove of outsider experience and making claims about our trans lives, our place in the world, and perhaps, our necessity as breath-embodied images of an eternally creative Divine Imaginary. But there is so much to say about such things. And, certainly, I do not presume to be the only one among us thinking, writing, and speaking these revelations into our collective imagining. *So, I will start with this:*

This book, this particular iteration of Trans-Forming Proclamation, is a kind of hybrid—equal parts story-telling, first-person theological propositions; assertions of the importance of gender-transcendence and expansiveness to a broader understanding of humanity; interpretations of scriptures foundational to such assertions; and a proposed theory and methodology for engaging transformed and informed testimonies, truth-claims, and faith-claims. While I am drawing on multiple ways of doing scholarship, engaging reflective interpretations, and making claims about particular experiences in a common human lot, this book is not an academic project. In fact, I am, with intention and forethought, turning aside from traditionally accepted and favored academic scholarly tropes, formulas, and ways of seeking validation.

I intend to engage, propose, and lift-up *other* ways of knowing, *other* ways of doing scholarship, *other* ways of theorizing and making informed assertions, in addition to and informing more traditional forms of study. If this work finds readership in the halls of academia, if it offers insights and inspirations to our would-be allies, accomplices, and co-conspirators, that is all well and good. However, these pages—these offerings of inquiries and propositions—are observations and reflections *for* our shared communities, specifically, for all of us transgender, non-binary, gender non-conforming, and intersex relations. This book is full of things that I long to lay open like a furrow of soil, like the crystals of a geode, that we might see together not only that which is normally hidden, but also all the potentialities and possibilities within it.

These movements, my searchings, captured in words here, are for us, for my kinfolk—for all of us who seek some sense of place or grounding in the faith systems that have tried to deny us, exclude us, vilify us, or erase us. These reflections are for those of us who search the dusty ground of our faith, grasping still for inklings of wisdom. The world *needs* us. The world *needs* our searching proclamations.

In the most bare and basic way, I am proposing something more than a little radical: that we outcasts, we misfits, *specifically* are invited, perhaps even *called*. We are called to do this work of liberation-seeking, faith-way-making *primarily* and *precisely* because we are cast-out from the places and spaces that house the self-appointed keepers and hoarders of religious teaching, faith-forming, and assumed access to Holiness (as if that can be contained and apportioned to others). All that is Good and Holy has invited *us* to create our own ground-up, tradition-transformations, to build our own thought-worlds and methodologies, to design our own systems of accountability for developing sound theories about the needful things.

In other words, we are called to offer our own *proclamations* about things that matter. I am claiming that we are invited by our own faith and by the God of the outcasts. Indeed, I am proclaiming that we are called, by and for one another, to make new meaning and to lift up new ideas *without* first seeking permission from well-meaning "allies," *without* first proving ourselves at the gates of academia, and *without* needing to apologize for doing so. Indeed, we must presume to speak for ourselves, because who else could possibly speak for us?

What I mean to say is that as we study, as we read our sacred texts (whichever ones we read), as we process the experiences of our lives, and as we pray—sometimes sobbing, sometimes in tongues others do not comprehend; sometimes dancing or shouting; sometimes sitting quietly on park benches or walking forest trails; sometimes before or after a meal; sometimes with the wordless prayers of our whole hearts—our sense of God discerned from an undeniable presence abides. Our own *experience* is more than sufficient.

It is more than possible—and even likely—that new life-changing and world-changing things come, not only from regurgitating and reprocessing the ideas of deceased patriarchs and occasional matriarchs, but even more so through bold, deliberate, thoughtful study, reflection, discernment, and proclamation by those among us now. That said, it is also good and helpful to read and consider, to contend with, and even wrestle with the works of those who have come before us. However, such supplications are not necessary for engaging our own experience, the sacred texts of our own lives, and the practices of our faith systems (if we have one) in relationship to our truth-claims. We can and must speak the revelations we discern through the living of our lives.

This book also engages an ongoing process of lifting-up, affirming, and celebrating who we are as gender-transcendent persons, our unique and needful place in the world, and our decidedly significant place in a wildly diverse, Eden-recalling sacred unfolding of a natural order, which proclaims Holy Otherness. Therefore, this book is, in subtle ways, a discussion or a dialogue. It is my effort to be personally engaged with you, my kindred. I am striving to do the work of Trans-Forming Proclamation that I am also *describing* in this book. In the process, I am also inviting a measure of creativity through my own use of images, word-play, turns of phrase, metaphors, and allegories—achieving, I hope, a certain prose poetics, even in the story-telling and scriptural explorations. In the work of creating our own ways of knowing, doing scholarship, and developing meaning-making methodologies, we are also free to embrace and express our own creative impulses.

I have sought to lead my mind with my heart. My hope is that you will meet me in that opening—in the space that vulnerability, outreach, and engagement create. I do not speak for others or attempt to speak for all of us; rather, I am attempting to speak *with* us—to make and hold space for us to be, share, dream, and proclaim together. I am daring to be fully present here with you—heart, mind, and body, expressed in the framework of these written words.

I want to be clear: I do not write as an authority or some singular *knower* above others. I am, in truth, more than a little suspicious of those who claim to be *knowers*—as I have seen, and still bear my own scars from, the harm *convinced-knowers*, in all their convictions, can do. I am also aware that, in this, I am far from alone. I write as one *knower* among many; as one *among* you—who are also knowers of your own internal sense of Sacred Abiding, experts in your own lived experience, makers of your own holy proclamations.

I do not know very many things for certain, but I believe this for sure: that this Holy Thing we call God—this sustaining, abiding, life-giving, and life-shaping Presence—does, indeed, come to us *everywhere*. The gifts that come from recognizing or from finding are actually born from our own seeking, questioning, and struggling.

So, this project aims to engage, and to perform—that is, to *do*—the things proposed within it. It is, as such, a kind of introduction to its own process, the process of doing Trans-Forming Proclamation. There is, to be sure, a foundational theological perspective and methodology at work in this book. However, I am not writing for scholarly affirmation. Those who are steeped in the methods and practices put forth in academic halls may notice and identify familiar theological and theoretical themes. However, while I believe that my underlying assumptions deserve scholarly attention, that conversation is ancillary to both my process and my proclamations.

In terms of format, the chapters in this book work through a kind of unfolding, presenting images, building a framework of ideas, and then reflecting on the assumptions and propositions of that framework. The primary image that shapes the claims made in this project center around the idea of the Sacred Grove, our origins in it, and implications for the overarching propositions of Trans-Forming Proclamation. The single most academic chapter—though it, too, is not traditionally academic—is the final chapter. In a sense, it is summarial. However, it is my hope that the final chapter will be almost unnecessary, if I have laid out an independent, robust, and cogent gender, theological, and justice-seeking theory and methodology, demonstrated prior to fully explaining it. At the end of the book, I have included an appendix of suggested resources for use in studying the religious texts shared, primarily, by Judaism and Christianity.

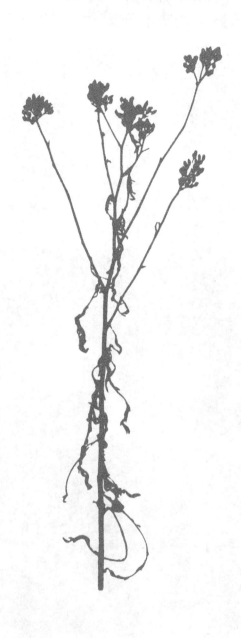

chapter one

Daring Existence

> *Then, God, the Eternal One, formed the earth-*
> *being from the dust of the ground and breathed into*
> *[their] nostrils the breath of life, and [they]*
> *became a living being. And God, the Existing One,*
> *planted a garden in Eden, eastward, and there God put the*
> *earth-being which God had formed.*
> **Genesis 2:7–8**
> **author's translation**

> *Before I formed you in the body, I knew you;*
> *before you left the womb, I sanctified you*
> *and I have given you, as a prophet, to the nations.*
> **Jeremiah 1:5**
> **author's translation**

The existence, the continual presence, of gender transcendence—of transgender, non-binary, gender non-conforming, and intersex persons in all our boldly particular personhood—testifies and proclaims. By this I mean, contrary to what we are too often told, our very presence in the world of persons is living testimony to the miraculous, co-creative, chrysaloid nature of human beingness and potentiality. Everywhere we are, there will also be the breathtaking fact of our existence.

What I mean to say is this: the moment we discern that our sense of gender-self is not congruent with the gender assigned to us and,

1

then, give ourselves permission to do whatever is necessary to actualize a more congruent selfhood, we engage an ongoing, evolving process of enacting, verbalizing, and living proclamations. When we begin wearing clothing that fits who we discern ourselves to be, we testify. When we change the way we wear our hair; when we augment aspects of our bodies; when we diminish features of our bodies; when we otherwise alter our bodies to reflect back to us—and others—who we understand ourselves to be; we make proclamations. When we choose a name that fits us, we speak who we are. When we claim and take actions to live into the sex we choose as self-affirming, rather than the sex chosen for us, we testify. Every movement we make toward fulfilling an authentic sense of self proclaims. Everything we do to live more honestly, comfortably, and congruently in our own skin sings psalms and shouts testimonies to the audaciously diverse, sacred nature of becoming.

Our embodied, enduring presence speaks, for we persist. Our presence testifies. Sometimes, we testify with words as well. Sometimes, in shouts; sometimes, in whispers; sometimes, even, in songs. We also have stories to tell. But, always, our insistent, defiant presence proclaims.

We are boundary-crossing beings. The eternal Grove breathes within us. This is so because, like all things—and certainly, all miraculous beings—we are born, first, within the great Divine Imaginary, the Grove-ground of being where all the distinctiveness and vitality of life originates and comes into existence. What I mean to say is that we are distinctly individuated images of our Creator's endlessly manifesting imagination—a vision of continual unfolding; seeded in freedom to become, rooted in diverse particularity bursting forth through us in curious and complex living landscapes; manifested in bodies burgeoning with selfhood, longing to be expressed and actualized. And yet, our existence in the earthly world posits us in a realm of human constructs that, ironically, lifts up the inherent diversity of the natural world and simultaneously dreads the naturally occuring differentiation of human beings.

That is, we are, all of us, Grove-born beings who, as soon as we begin toddling about, are thrust into a world formed around humanly crafted interpretations of the natural world bent on conforming all that is into narrowly contrived ideas of how everything—and every human being—ought to be. To guide us toward conformity, we are enculturated toward a singular, supposedly natural and normal human form: a human-made doppelganger. Everything around us mirrors back to us this image of a universal human, complete with prescribed attributes, characteristics, and valued qualities. Anything that deviates from this singular image is deemed an anomaly, at best, and an abomination, at worst. Differentiation is tolerated inasmuch as an individual remains in some similitude of the culturally cultivated norm. Individuality is framed and worshiped within controlled variations of a straw person—like a child's clay doll, formed from the weak reeds, stagnant mud, thorny briars, and weeds in a fabricated garden. The lazy overlords who built this pretensive, faux garden believe dominion is the way to beat back their primal, insecure fear of what might be—what might, without prevention, emerge. They fear imagination.

In this mythological world, in this place of unimagining, likeness is sameness. Gardens are framed and contained by brick and mortar, sidewalks, roadways, and cities—because that which does not fit the constructed golems of the world must be contained. Meanwhile, groves are abandoned, erased, obscured. That which does not fit the revered universal doppelganger troubles those who no longer remember they, too, are born from, and into, a vast, unfettered continual unfolding of divine creation.

Thus, we are born into a world that is both ill-prepared for us and fundamentally frightened of us, as individuals, and also of all we represent collectively. To survive this world with any hope of flourishing, we draw upon and learn to perfect specialized, adaptive capacities. We learn to attune all our senses, like a compass, toward our internal "true north" and move eastward toward the rising sun, whose light points us homeward. We spend our lives moving toward the indwelling, germinal garden of our personhood. We develop uncanny abilities for intuiting, nurturing, guarding, and protecting this garden, this sacred personhood that lives deep within us—even as we, paradoxically, live within it. Most surely, we discover ways to be in, but not of, the ill-suited world and to move through it. We learn to *find* and *create* our own life-ways. We discern and manifest how to make crossings between this ill-prepared, ill-suited world we inhabit and the innate, verdant world of our own sacred, Grove-born self-hood.

We are beings of boundary-thresholds and sacred *other-spaces*. We live ever at the thresholds created by forces outside of ourselves. We seek to find and create spaces within ourselves—and within re-lational community with others—to discern our own sense of per-sonhood. We seek, always, to cultivate and actualize our own sense of selfhood and to form spaces in which we can express who we are. We find ourselves living in a world of ill-fitting, unaccommodating encounters. This world demands that we find and cross into sanctu-ary-spaces where people who are also made "others" gather for shel-ter, support, and some measure of community. We redress, reshape, and transform our own body-spaces. We redress, reshape, and trans-form the spaces around us. We move adeptly, intuitively, between soul-crushing constrictive spaces constructed around us and life-af-firming other-spaces that foster personal discernment, actualization, growth, and trans-formation. We are always crossing thresholds.

These threshold spaces, these *other-spaces*, are anywhere and ev-erywhere gender-diverse and gender-expansive persons dare to live and move and have our being; this *everywhere* is *anywhere* we happen to be:

grocery stores, gas stations, hair salons, and barber shops;

classrooms, city council rooms, banks, ball fields, race tracks, and yard sales;

street corners, coffee houses, doughnut shops, bus stops, and homeless shelters;

queer bars, spoken-word slams, drag balls, and ice cream shops;

community gardens, parks, fishing holes, farms, and farmer's markets;

shopping malls, thrift stores, cycle shops, and hiking trails;

laundromats, living rooms, front-porch swings, and first-date
meeting spots;
recovery rooms, waiting rooms, dining rooms, hotel rooms, and
no-tell rooms;
synagogues, churches, temples, covens, sacred circles, mosques,
and meditation groups;
beaches, mountain trails, and sitting-on-the-back-porch stoops;
day cares, nursing homes, and happy, home-alone, thank-God-
I'm-on-my-own homes;
half-way houses, tree houses, ballroom houses, and not-quite-
mine-but-I'm-still-paying houses;
tattoo parlors, wide open fields, open-mic-night clubs, cruise
ships, and cruise strips;
sports bars, dining cars, pastry shops, bakeries, and cowboy bars;
cell phones, jail cells, counselor's couches, and sitting-in-my-den-
watching-tv couches;
check-out lines, day-labor lines, and putting-it-all-on-the-line
job-fair lines;
trailer parks, amusement parks, and loving-walking-with-sweet
heart parks;
libraries, book stores, music halls, crowded streets, quiet places,
and other-spaces.

Wherever we go, wherever we are, there will also be the breathtaking fact of our existence. This is our living proclamation. We are
the embodiment of the Sacred Grove, reverberating with the echo
of Life itself. We are diverse persons speaking entire storied worlds
through the moment-to-moment pulse of our lives.

We are an ancient people. Across time and history, gender-transcendent persons have been proclaiming resiliency: the fact of our
insistent, meaningful existence. As such, we have been speaking the
nuanced facts of personhood, of daring to *be* unique. This we have
done, and this we continue to do in defiant resistance to many and
various attempts to erase us—literally and figuratively, legally and
medically, physically and institutionally.

We have been here, roaming the earth, living, expressing, and,

5

thus, telling our various truths. We have been making significant contributions to our respective cultures for as long as there have been people. We have been called by many names. We have been holy people and healers; we have been vilified and burned on stakes—both literally and metaphorically.

We, as gender-transcendent persons, have even been treasurers for queens. No less than twelve eunuchs, we are told, served Queen Esther who, in her efforts to save the Jewish people, learned some things about "coming out" as requisite for living a righteous authenticity. Once, in other cultures and other times, we were indeed shamans and healers.

More recently in our history, we have been, and are, assistants to Congresspersons, advisors to Presidents, and elected officials. We have been and are doctors, nurses, lawyers, teachers, and preachers; we are siblings, parents, cousins, and children. We have been and are scholars, writers, poets, artists, musicians, and performers—sometimes, all of these at once.

Some of us are descendants of enslaved peoples and some descend from perpetrators of slavery, debased by the presumption that one human being can own and subjugate another. Some of us are indigenous First Peoples. Others of us share lineage with betrayers of First Peoples who condoned or actively perpetrated abuses, betrayals, and violence against Indigenous peoples. Some of us are descendants of the complicated intersections of these histories. That is, possibly, some of us descend from *both* enslaved peoples and slavers, from colonized peoples and colonizers (like me), and thus, we carry and hold all those tensions in our tender bodies. Some of us hail from far-off lands, and some of us have no permanent home. Some of us speak multiple languages. And some of us are not sure where we came from or exactly where we are going, but, nonetheless, we persevere.

We are students, landscape workers, and electricians. We are farm workers and trade workers getting by in non-traditional ways. We are thinkers, creators, community-builders, and organizers. We are cooks, chefs, candy-makers, and bread-bakers. We are ministers,

6

counselors, and sponsors. We are neighbors and co-workers. We are, some of us, still figuring out who we are and who we hope to be.

We have been revered and reviled. We have been fantasized about and feared. We have been—and still are—exoticized and exploited and equally ignored. We have been forced to live within—and to re-sist—equal measures of condemnation and commodification of our lives, our bodies, our stories, our gifts, our talents, and our contribu-tions. Still, we endure. We persist.

We have been here, always, living, creating, sharing, contribut-ing, proclaiming. In our passing, we leave behind the artifacts of our lives, which are our lived and living stories. We are an ancient, resil-ient, and persistent people. *Any and every place where trans persons dare to exist becomes an ever-speaking, Sacred Grove.*

The body speaks. We speak. In many, marvelous ways, we pro-claim.

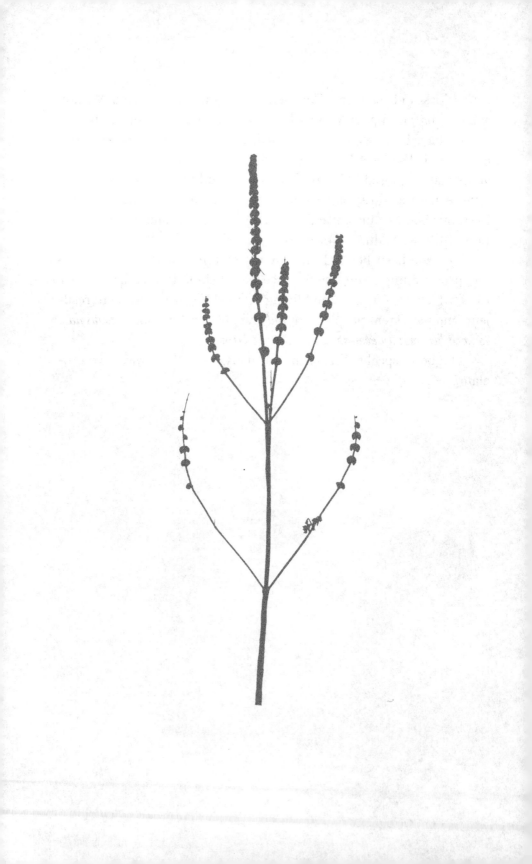

chapter two

Words Matter

And God said, "let there be light," and there was light.
Genesis 1:3
author's translation

Therefore, thus says the Existing One, God of hosts,
"because you have spoken this word, behold,
I am designating the words in your mouth to fire
and this people wood; it will consume them."
Jeremiah 5:14
author's translation

Throughout the centuries, across traditions, and in diverse ways, the sages have proposed that language, itself, is sacred. It is, they suggest, the means of making; the means, even, of prayer. Some say, before making worlds and beings, God's first creative act was to make the *means of creation*—letters, the makers of words; words, the substance of thought; words, the makers of meaning.[1]

In the beginning was *the Word*, so one story goes, and the word *was* God. Other stories suggest, God spoke this language God created, this holy utterance, and entire worlds came into being. The *God-Word*, present in worded being, earth and bone, water and skin,

---

1 Portions of this chapter pertaining to the idea that "words matter because words are matter" (the core of this chapter) arose from writing projects in which I engaged in early 2018 aimed toward this work and other worded dreams. Sections from that writing appeared in several speeches, or sermons, during and since that time. Portions appearing here fulfill the original purpose of those earlier writing projects.

sky and breath. Everywhere, God's thoughts, manifest in substance, form, and symbol. In a miraculous gift of hope-filled trust, God bestowed upon us, too, the capacity for language—for sounds, glyphs, signs, symbols, and signification: the stuff of creation.

Words matter, we could say, because words _are matter_. It is with the power of words in mind that I will consider the task of Trans-Forming Proclamation. What I mean to say: Words are living things, _spirits_ of a sort—transforming the continuous flow of synaptic activity into thoughts, ideas, beliefs—the electro-chemical matter of human meaning and motivation.

There is a kind of magic in our words that bears consideration. Words communicate. Words create and destroy. Words heal and words harm. Words shape and form destinies and words erase. Words frame and express emotions, desires, feelings, thoughts, beliefs, and sensations. Words make love and war, violence and compassion. Words insinuate and embed into beings, bodies, cultures, societies. Words marginalize and oppress ... and words create revolutions.

Words are the connective tissue of thought, experience, motivation, and behavior.

We are born into worlds built on words. Culture, itself, is crafted by lexicons of conscious and semi-conscious assumptions, paradigms, ideologies, and agreements; these, too, shape, form, and craft the social practices that, in turn, support and preserve them. Language, itself, is like bricks and mortar; it is neutral. The same bricks and mortar can be put to building a prison, a hospital, or a cathedral. Depending on the thought-worlds that create these spaces and those created within them, a cathedral can be a prison, or a prison can be a cathedral.

Whether words frame conditions of thriving or suffering depends on the ways in which language moves in a given culture, the ways in which it is used, and the meaning paradigms it builds and conveys—the ways in which the language of a social system works on and within us. This is to say: the systems, conditions, and institutions of any culture are the results of beliefs, values, ideologies, and paradigms that the language allows and enables human beings to create. As such, language itself may indeed be neutral, but the use of language is far from neutral. What we word into being—what we conjure in thoughts, beliefs, and values—conjures our individual and social behavior and manifests all the social and cultural paradigms, systems, and structures at work in the world we inhabit.

These days, every day, we are reminded how the powerful manipulate and pervert these paradigms: normalcy and deviance, male and female, natural and unnatural, heterosexual and otherwise-sexual, good and evil, race and whiteness, wealthy and working class, ability and disability, citizen and alien, privilege and exclusion, knowledge and facts, law and order, truth and lies. These, the stuff of ideologies brought low and active among us, call our attention to the ways we both *allow* and *participate in* ideologies that marginalize, oppress, and manifest fear and hatred of difference. We inherit a world of words and all the stuff those words make and unmake. What we conjure becomes, equally, the means of care and flourishing or the means of deprivation and marginalization—and all that lies between.

All this is complicated by an obvious fact: what we conjure with our words exists within and arises out of what already exists. The means available to us for this process of wording and meaning-making are, at once, already given to us and comprise, also, the stuff from which we make new—or, at least, describe and clarify what we have been given. We are drinking, so to speak, from the very water we are trying to unpollute, refresh, and renew.

Words matter because words *are matter*: the sticks and stones that harm us; the brick and mortar of empires; the cages of internment camps; the ropes and chains of enslavement; the foundations of oppression, and even, it seems, the blueprints, plans, and building blocks of liberation, healing, and flourishing.

Throughout this work, I am often making use of certain pre-existing words, so I want to be clear about what I mean when I use them. I also want to acknowledge that many of these words are far from perfect. It is also true our words for ourselves are changing all the time. I am aware not everyone will like, appreciate, or agree with words I use, just as there are words used in our communities that do not speak to me. My hope is that the words I choose to use will be the least offensive or aggravating options among the imperfect vernacular available to us. My intention is not to elevate or to privilege one term over another; my aim is to communicate for the sake of—and in the hope of—shared understanding.

When I use the term "trans," I am employing it as a recognized, admittedly imperfect, shorthand umbrella term intended to acknowledge and refer all of us whose gender self-understanding is incongruent with the gender assigned to us at birth. Therefore, this term attempts to capture all of us along a marvelously diverse, inward-outwardly spiraling gender-identity spectrum, to include persons among us who may claim any, or all, of the following self-identifications: transgender, gender queer, gender-fluid, non-binary, agender, omnigender, transsexual, gender non-conforming, two spirit, and a whole host of other creative, personally-crafted (or culturally honored) gender descriptive terms that assist us in naming our gender identities. When I use the generally accepted term "transgender," I am employing that word in the same way, as an imperfect, recognizable term preferred by a measurable number of us (but, also, equally dissatisfying to a fair number of us). When I use the term "intersex" I am respectfully acknowledging persons whose physical body manifests somewhere along a vast range of embodied presentations and experiences of chromosomal combinations, reproductive capacities, primary and secondary sex characteristics, and expressions that do not fall neatly into the arbitrary and reductive classifications of "male" and "female" sex expectations.

On one level, the ways in which I am employing language in this book is a direct, intentional response to the ways in which words have been used against us and have, in fact, created us. That is to say: those of us who are gender-transcendent persons have been worded into identities that we are then compelled to claim, assert, express, and—too often—defend. Were it not for the word-paradigms that, over the centuries, shaped and crafted the reductive sex and gender binaries that define us in the negative, by exclusion, we would not be forced into seeking language and creating words to define ourselves—who we are—in the positive. If oppressive, exclusionary binaries did not exist, we would no doubt be defining ourselves as something else. We would be seen by others as some other kinds of persons.

Because we do not, yet, live in a world liberated from reductive, exclusionary sex and gender binary systems—or any other binaries, for that matter—we do not know what that something other-than transgender, non-binary, and/or intersex might be. I would like to imagine, however, we would exist in a world-space (and word-space) that allowed us to simply be persons—free to be, love, create, contribute, thrive, and become, living on in all our glorious, gender-transcendent beingness and particular personhoods. Who knows? In such a world we might, even and again, be shamans, healers, and wise people as we once were, long ago, in diverse cultures throughout the world. But, I digress, as I am prone to do, and have lapsed into dreaming dreams of the liberated days to come, for which we hope and work.

When I make use of hyphenated, imaginary-making, word-crafting terms, I am doing so in response to my own continuing, searching desire for more expansive, descriptive, accepting, and affirming language—language that is more joy-filled and does good beyond simply expanding our range of academic classifications. I engage my own, likely inadequate, wordsmithing inclinations, in order to push the language we are given in an ever-hopeful attempt at breaking open that which we have inherited. We have been conditioned to think and operate in very limited ways—and it takes creative energy, trial and error to free ourselves from those limitations.

Therefore, I make use of word-phrases such as gender-expansive, gender-diverse, gender-resisting, gender-transforming, gender-transgressing, and a host of others. Of late, I have come to hold a preference for using the term "gender-transcendent" to describe not only the many and unfolding identities we embody within Creator's vast, evolving, endlessly diverse pandimensional realm of persons, but also to push forward, actively engage, and model a call to continually reimagine what it means to live, move, and have our being as human persons. Such imagining and reimagining is, essentially, trans-dimensional: that is, it is at once earth-bound and transcendent; fundamentally embodied and also deeply spiritual; intuitively mystical and relentlessly practical. Seeking to become ourselves in such an intentional way is not only engaged to make manifest who we are, but also a striving toward who we hope to be.

For many of us, this pursuit, this longing to be seen and received in community as our most authentic selves, is religious or spiritual. At the core, such lived imagining is an ongoing, dynamic engaging of predispositions, intuitions, choices, discernments, values, dreams, and desires manifesting in various personal expressions of embodied sovereignty, meaning-making, and authenticity. This is the imagining our very presence in the world proclaims and invites us *all* to engage. In other words, this striving, this longing, this becoming, is not unique to gender-transcendent people. It is a fundamentally human experience, even if the details may not be the same.

The point is this: words matter. How words are used matters. The need to continually upend, turn inside-out, reframe, reclaim, and revise existing word paradigms remains. I purposely engage in word play, intentionally wording charms of making to counter the charms of un-making worded against us. I strive to conjure images and exchanges, potential inspirations, and perhaps, some degree of healing and renewal to ward off the harmful thought-worlds that confine us. I do this with awareness of the ways in which our ancestors before us also worded new life into their circumstances and of the shared language that remains as their legacy. I seek to honor that tradition and to extend it. I know that I am not alone in this effort and trust that my failures will be corrected by those who come after me.

Words matter because words *are* matter.

I am striving to use words in ways that invoke meaning-making while actively challenging inherited assumptions, and intentionally lifting-up renewed imaginaries. I am making conjures of my own. In the process, I am returning to, rereading, and reimagining thought worlds we have been given. I am also intentionally upending language, assumptions, and traditions about who God is, who we are, who is privileged to think and speak about God, and who can make proclamations.

Any offense caused through my use of language is most assuredly unintentional. And, no doubt, any inspiration, hopefulness, comfort, or insight found in these words results from some combination of cosmic, holy-happenstance and an earnest but imperfect striving to look and listen deeply, to question and seek some growth-facilitating understanding in myself, others, and the world around me. Of the two poles of possibility, my hope is for the latter.

chapter three

Our Stories about God

And God answered Moses,
"I Shall Be As I Shall Be"/"I Am Who I Am."
And God said: "So shall you say to the
children of Israel, 'I Shall Be has sent me to you.'"
Exodus 3:14
author's translation

Talking about God is messy. Uncomfortable. Even troubling. It is especially so for us as people toward whom God has been weaponized, as surely as biblical scripture has been harmfully directed at us—used, in fact, not only to negate, or erase, our existence, but to vilify us and relegate us to the status of sinful, willful abominations. We have been, in multiple ways, offered up on the anti-altars of religious traditions that conflate God with scriptures about God and, worse, conflate God with self-proclaimed people of God.

Words *are* matter. And the words about God, mistaken for the *being* of God, have been forged into the work of our various oppressions. Harm has been done. Harm is still being done. Resultantly, shimmering streams of some discernible truths about human experiences of God are obscured in the matter.

Given these realities, it seems pertinent to explore, for a moment, the set of perplexing and often troubling images that arise, as well as the life-giving potentialities that emerge, when the word *God* is invoked. I am hinting at who, or what, God might be by making proclamations—as well as hinting at what and who God most certainly is

17

not. Most notably, I suggest that God is not merely a supernatural, super-version of a universal human. God is not us. And we most surely are not God. And so, the age-old question emerges: who, or what, is God? This is an important point of reflection.

Most fundamentally, many of us gender-transcendent folks see or hear the word *god* and are immediately presented with images of the supernatural Force behind everything that has been manipulated and used—with varying degrees of controlling mal-intent, harm, abuse, and violence—against us. For many among us, *"god"* is a punishing, hateful, harsh, fickle, and self-contradicting entity whose supposed love for us is far from what we imagine love to be. This "god" is a mean-spirited, manipulator-god: a source of shame, inducing self-loathing and a pervasive, internalized sense of wrongness. This "god" is also, ironically, inconsistent with the images of some Sacred Presence expressed, specifically, in the spirit of Jewish and Christian sacred texts. This "god" is a false god; the "god" of fearful anti-love.

But, blessed be the wounded children of this anti-God, those who lived before, and those living still—those who survived in the past, and those still surviving the wounding, and in doing so, finding something within themselves, and perhaps beyond, worth holding on to and believing in. Blessed be those who found healing, those healing still, and especially, those who may never fully heal, but still persist in living on. Blessed be their lives, for their living-on reminds us to search for the *other* Many-Named, One God; the Holy Something above and beyond a troublingly human false "god"—the Something More, the God of the Othered, who abides; the God of the beloved, sacred wounded-ones, who sustains.

For others of us, the term "god" implies yet another human construct, created to offer some explanation for things unexplainable, and a modicum of comfort in trouble, to our ancestors who described this god and, even, to many in our time. To some, the idea of "god" is nothing more than a nice, perhaps moderately comforting, but nonetheless simplistic idea. This "god," we might propose, is the God of doubt. Blessed be the doubters, for they offer a tender, inviting hand, leading a way out of the narrow darkness of unquestioning, unexamined, acquiescence to the smooth comfort of familiarity and hab-it. And, blessed be the God who not only allows but invites doubt, knowing better than we that a measure of doubt is essential to a movement from mere belief to a meaningful, enlivened, and sustain-ing faith. Doubt calls forth the possibility that the way toward the Unknowable-Knowable One is found along the winding path run-ning right through the middle of our own *unknowing.*

There are also those among us for whom the term *God* is com-forting and precious, as it names the living God of our experience; the God who sustained and accompanied us, never leaving us amid the harm caused by members of the self-proclaimed *people of God,* the saints; the self-appointed knowers and keepers of righteousness. This "god," without doubt, is the God of miraculous experience—the God who sustains all by actively loving all, *even* those whose idea of God, and of love, is hard, arrogant, cruel, and rejecting; blessed be the God who comforts the hurt and rejected ones and reminds us all that God is *not* God's people. And, blessed be the hurt and rejected ones, for they teach us to hold on another day and to trust, above all else, the indwelling sense of God that is real and present within us.

For some of us, all these experiences of "god," and God's pro-fessed people, have been, and are still, our own experiences as well. Others of us have more personal connections, and disconnections, to some idea of "god" not named here (it is impossible to name them all; better to leave some things unsaid than to do harm by misrepre-sentation). So, blessed be unmentioned experiences. For that which is deeply private teaches us about sacred boundaries, about what is shared well in community and what is not—and about honoring the quiet presence of that which is close, intimate; undisclosed.

For some of us, there is not one "god," but many. Blessed be the holders of many Gods, for they teach us to expand our recognition of multiple experiences and varied paths to multiplicities of truth. The followers of many Gods call into being a wider, broader, and deeper visioning, not only of Sacred Presence, but of the many and varied ways some holy Presence manifests in the lives of others, guiding us to see multiple manifestations of Holiness in our own lives. And, blessed be the Many Gods who remind us there truly is one river and many wells.

For others still, there simply is no idea of "god" that works for them, no words, no descriptors because, for them, there simply is no "god." Blessed be the children of no-god, for their unbelief informs recognition of what is not-God, opening a way to more profound, deeper faith; their no-god teaches us to imagine, deeply, who God might be through who God most surely is not, and to imagine ways God speaks, even through silence.

In previous chapters, I have already made statements conveying some of my own thinking about who God might be and likely is not. I will continue to do so, as engaging questions about God and seeking after tell-tale signs, glimpses, and possible insights in religious texts, experiences of bodied self, others, and the world describe and demonstrate the project of Trans-Forming Proclamation. However, I do not—as centuries of, predominantly, Christian thinkers have done—presume to assert that my perspectives and faith claims are the absolute, definitive, or only, truth-claims about God. It would be preposterous to claim to know, definitively, who God is, and especially so, to claim to know for all people, in all times, places, cultures, circumstances, and ranges of experiences. But, it is possible to work with the faith claims we have been given, inquiring, searching, and discerning insights about the possible nature of God, God's relationship to us, and ours to God. It is possible to engage in breaking open our sacred texts, experiences shared and passed on; our personal and communal experiences; the world of human conditions and history, too; and to process these through all the ways of knowing, discerning, questioning, and developing descriptions available to us. I am offering one way of doing this. I am most decidedly sure there are many other ways.

Ultimately, I am proposing that what we have been given—the collections of stories accessible and familiar to most of us raised in Christendom—is a collection of stories that tell us *not*, definitely or absolutely, who God *is*, but rather who God *may be experienced and discerned to be*, which may also point us toward understanding who

God is not. I am also asserting, throughout, that the stories we have been given, these texts we deem sacred, speak to us valuable pieces and parts of a larger, overarching, still-being-written story of humanity's inquiry into, and search for understanding of, the God of human experience. Said another way: the stories we have been given are part of an ongoing, cumulative experience of God, among and with, particular people, in specific places, conditions, and cultures, who assumed there is a God, experienced this God in their lives and history, and were so impacted by those experiences they were compelled to document and pass on to us their experiences. Thus, these stories tell us more about *how* God has been *experienced* than about absolute definitions of who, or what, God is. And yet, equally, these collections of experiences teach us about God; about how the presence of this assumed and felt *Something More* we call God can be felt, discerned, and experienced, again and anew, in the receiving of these stories and the making of our own.

As such, the stories in our sacred texts offer a *spiritual history* of people who lived in a world where the being of God was assumed, experienced a presence they recognized as God, and participated in an ongoing search for relationship with, and greater understanding of, the Divinity they experienced. Thus, our sacred texts are stories of the human search for God born in experiences that may inspire us to believe there must be God and create desire to know this Presence-Force more relationally. What is discovered in that searching, indeed, contributes to a measure of understanding who God is, how God is present, felt, and experienced, and how God moves and acts within and among us. Therefore, in every way we sense the presence of God, search for greater connection to God, and pass on to one another—perhaps, to our communities and our world—our experiences of this Divine Presence, we contribute to this ongoing, cumulative, grander story of who *we are*, as human beings, in search of and in relation to a Many-Named God. Perhaps, too, we contribute to the story of who God is in search of us and in relation to us.

That said, when I use the term *God*, I am aware it is a term, not the entity, or being, to which it refers. And yet, it *is* a word that

21

matters because it *is* a kind of matter—a word that conjures; a word imbued with meanings, implications, and associations beyond the *Something* it seeks to describe. It is a weighty term, packed with all manner of tangible harm, hurt, healing, sorrow, longing, revelations, possibilities, prayers, frustrations of prayers, horrors, joys, celebrations, and more still—all coexisting together, conjuring sensations, feelings, emotions, thoughts, doubts, and proclamations. All of this accompanies all the thought-worlds and endeavors in this work.

So, aware of these realities, when I use the term *God* I do so to reframe and re-contextualize appropriations of this word we have suffered and are still suffering. That is, I am intentionally using the word to compare and contrast, define and redefine, refute and re-place, in a sense, descriptions of "God" that do not seem to be God-like, to turn a phrase. When I use the word *God* I am referring to the idea of an existing, eternal, force-presence that is transcendent yet knowable and felt; beyond, yet experientially engaged with and relational to human beings. Like our ancestors before us, I am also assuming that this Presence possesses and expresses attributes, qualities, and dispositions that we sense experientially, personally, and sometimes collectively. I am, then, employing the process expressed in Trans-Forming Proclamation to reflect on, inquire about, and hopefully discern gleanings about the possible nature of this Something More and who this Sacred Presence might be—and most especially, who we, as gender-transcendent persons, might be in relation to this Presence-Force, to one another, and to the world we inhabit.

chapter four

Sacred Grove, Living Proclamation

And I will return the captives, my people, Israel.
And they will rebuild the desolated cities
and dwell in them; and they will plant vineyards
and drink the wine, and make gardens and eat the fruit.

Amos 9:14
author's translation

And the Eternal One will guide you continually and
satisfy your soul in scorched places, and strengthen your bones;
and you will be like a watered garden, and like
a spring of water whose waters do not fail.

Isaiah 58:11
author's translation

For as long as we can ascertain human existence, groves have been places of proclamation. From the earliest humans circled round a crackling fire to Druid Groves; from gatherings of wise people across time and cultures, dancing in ancient tree-bordered clearings marked with moonlit standing stones and sacred springs, to earth and stone henges, medicine wheels, Antebellum "hush harbor" gatherings of enslaved peoples and the "arbor churches" born during the Great Awakenings, the grove has been a place of worship, prayer, and proclamation. The Grove is an enduring allegory. By this I mean, it is both a symbolic image—and real expression—of multiple truth-bearing realities.

On one level, a grove represents a gathering of persons who have, in one way or another, been called—and often, driven—to the safety of the hidden grove. The Sacred Grove is a place where people gather for community, strength, shared identity, communal celebration, and more. The Sacred Grove is set apart for sanctuary, solidarity, and resistance.

The Grove, as allegory, is also archetypal. Primal. Primitive and permeated with transcendence. Something deep in the belly of our collective unconsciousness, low in our limbic systems, feels the call of the Grove. An ancient memory recognizes the footfalls of our ancestors, senses the drumbeat rhythm of their beingness and experiences in history. Across time, they beckon to us and we follow. As we consent to the inner summons of selfhood, we circle round the Sacred Grove, dancing the interweaving, inward-outward dance of becoming. We proclaim. There, in that equally real and *other*-worldly place, we meet all our relations in a marvelous, mysterious connectedness. We meet each other as kin. We meet the earth, as we plant ourselves firmly. Claiming our true selves, we greet ourselves. Perhaps, more than merely this (though this is more than enough), we also meet the known-yet-unknowable Spirit who calls each of us into being.

In every breath, in every intuitive, purposeful movement toward our fullest selves and our hopeful flourishing, our beingness proclaims something profound and eternal: the bare, coexisting, reality of life; the audacity of breath-invigorated existence; the persistence of personhood daring to be and to become.

The Grove of which I speak is sacred space. It speaks. Sometimes, in whispers. Nonetheless, it speaks.

The bordering trees and all that nests and feeds within them; the grasses, the insects and creeping, crawling things; the wild flowers, bushes, brambles, and thickets at the boundaries; the four-legged creatures whose varied hooved, padded, clawed, and cloven feet grace the ruddy earth; mosses, fallen leaves, and wandering mounded mole trails; the winged creatures flying above; the surrounding rocks, streams, and forest-shadowed, rain-soaked puddles—the twigs, broken branches, rotting stumps, and decaying things; even worms and ant hills; the gathering of all these and more; even the deer, eyes flashing in the moonlit night; the whole community of all our relations, entire, speaks.

The fact of existence, of enduring presence, testifies.

Every being, every*thing*—every atom-made, molecule-manifesting, compound-consisting thing—proclaims not only, or merely, the marvelously intelligent, interdependent diversity of creation, but equally and profoundly, the fundamental and persistently *particular is-ness of being*.

The fact of existence proclaims.

The Grove speaks. Sacred syllables burst forth in the very being of it. Sometimes, in whispers. Sometimes in shouts, even in song; sometimes in silence. Nonetheless, the Grove speaks. And so, too, do we—equally earth-bound, wildly unique, gender-diverse human beings. For we, too, persist.

Within the Sacred Grove, there is no apologetic defense. No justification for being. There is only the bareness of life; the insistence of being; the earthly reality of dust-formed begotten-ness, being and becoming; the persistent pulse of existence before an abiding, eternal, many-named Creator.

The Grove is liminal. It is the place where the extraordinary is revealed in the ordinary—where the unusual, the odd, the strange, perhaps even the freakish and absurd, points a slender, fleshy finger toward assumptive constructions of what is and is not natural. It is, itself, transitional space. It is a barely perceptible, yet palpable place; a strangely moveable midpoint between the here-and-now and the yet-be-realized; a shimmery, half-light presence between the *something-more* and the mundane, where earthbound embodied being and some *other-ness* connect, revealing the undeniable, essential bond between them. The Grove exists just over the threshold-space we step lightly and decidedly across, one foot on the firm fecund ground, the other in the equally embodied, equally sensual, inexplicably transcendent *other*-space of gender-transcendent presence. And, there, we remember: these are inseparable.

Grove and threshold are intimately bound, like ocean and marshland; river and riverbank, each always bearing something of the other. Grove-born beings are, naturally, diverse and expansive manifestations of all that is life-expressive. Everywhere around us is the thin, mystical borderland between the ancient embryonic Grove and everything else. We are people of the primeval Grove living in the brick-and-mortar world of human ideas and constrictions. We are walkers of the threshold between the germinal Grove of originations and everywhere else. We are movers between worlds. We are always crossing over.

As diverse, gender-transcendent people, we intuit this. *Know* it. In our skin. Even when we cannot find words to articulate it, even if we name it other things, this arcane *knowing* resides in us. The Grove is in us. We are in the Grove. Born of the Grove, travelers of the world, we live, always, at the thresholds. We are people of the boundaries between continual, expansive *becoming* and the static world of contrived absolutes around us.

We do not choose to be called—to be drawn, enfleshed skin, bone, blood, spirit—into this body-bound yet trans-mundane *other*-space, this space of being beyond what is prescribed, what is allowed; but we *do*, most surely, *choose* to *enter*. To step lightly across the threshold. To live and move and have our being in transit, waking and sleeping, being, doing, and dreaming in the in-between. In so doing, we testify. We proclaim the persistent is-ness of personhood in the *other*-space and simultaneously, always, in *this* space; the space we inhabit: the place where everywhere we are is liminal crossing. Where everywhere we are is a continual moving to and from the ground of embryonic existence and the imposed concreteness of the world, from who we are through and over who we are told we can be, and back to self, again. One foot here and one foot there, we are in the Grove and the Grove is in us. Everywhere we are is Sacred Grove, speaking—sometimes, in whispers—the insistent fact of existence. *Our* existence.

In other stories, in other times, the Grove might be called *the garden*. Eden, perhaps. Whether we call it grove, garden, or something else, it remains the barely perceptible, still-here and yet-to-come everyplace and no-place where all that lives persists in marvelously unique manifestations of the active principle of creation, discerned and expressed in all our religion. What I mean to say is that creation—as our sacred stories imply—is not a single event, lost to us in the before-time. Creation is continual, infinite, and expansive rather than restrictive; it is also cumulative. That is, creation arises out of creation; it is a continuing process that creates out of, and from the stuff of, itself. Each of the six days of creation are foundational, life-giving movements in the perpetual unfolding of the process-forces of creation. Each movement, and manifestation of life brought forth within them, is connected and foundational to all the subsequent movements. The interdependence of creation unfolds within the interdependence of unfolding days, circumstances, forces, and beings.

Even the ever-recurring sabbath is created, and given shape and form, by the six days that preceded it. The Sabbath is that original moment-space in which God ceased from working, took a breath with the whole of creation, and refreshed—literally, re-souled, in the Hebrew (*vayinafash*)—Godself; and it is equally and simultaneously, that original collection of sanctuary moments in time and every Sabbath moment since and yet to come. Yet, the Sabbath does not exist, nor does it have meaning, without the cumulative, revolving six days that precede it—or, it could be said, without the eighth day that follows and, then, becomes the first day, again.

I digress here, to assert that the underlying principle of creation is continual, diversity-drenched, interconnected and individuated, cumulative unfolding that arises from the elements of creation, itself. And more, to propose that the Grove, too, is a space in time, like the Sabbath, where all that is, was, and is yet to come, takes a moment and breathes a soul-quenching, renewing breath together with Creator. The Grove, then, is equally—like the Sabbath—a sanctuary in time. It is a space that exists, at once, in the before-time, in this time, and in all times to come. The Sacred Grove gives sanctuary to all who dare to exist and strive to flourish in bodied identities that push against, resisting, the contrived constrictive norms crafted in the world of human constructs. It is the space where all who have been made *other*, who have been pushed outside, enter in, take a re-souling breath and find, within, the strength and wherewithal to make for themselves a selfhood that harms none, gives meaning to their lives, and makes their living-on worth doing.

The Grove is the space where embodiment and spirit come together in the now. It is, itself, simultaneously an *other-space* burgeoning with unfettered *being* and, equally, the birthplace of naturally remarkable persons whose notable particularity—even strangeness, weirdness, or perceived freakishness—is intolerable to the narrow, insecure world of human un-imagining. What I mean to say is this: human insecurity, fear of difference, suspiciousness of novelty, and the need to simulate security and exercise power through all manner of imposed sameness have produced an opposing force to imagination; a kind of anti-matter, *active un-imagining* that seeks, self-consciously, to obscure, if not undo, the free, unbridled, ever-emerging diversity of creation, entire. To box it up. Contain it. Control and restrict the very elements, materials, and forces of life.

As surely as generations of humans have imagined God in self-referencing, self-reflecting ways—much too small and confining for any being who is truly God to conform to or inhabit—humans have un-imagined the whole of humanity into a narrow, homogeneous, personhood-choking image, and then, consigned us all to conform to it and live in it. Or, if not, to be deemed freak, abomination, pervert, hopeless sinner, or all of these and worse. Yet, within the Grove, the persistence of boldly brave and individuated, weirdly strange, wonderfully freakish, beautiful beings points a knowing finger and lifts a winking gaze all the way back to Eden—where the stuff of everything that was, is and ever will be, was born.

The Sacred Grove is also the sanctuary space where all of us who are made *other* are driven. It is the *any-place* we create—together or alone—crossing over from the chaos of the world into the assurance of selfhood and, there, take in a fuller, deeper breath. It is the space of origination and becoming where we take a rest, renew, refresh. It is the place imperceptible to those who have never, by longing and necessity, learned to seek it, peer through the veil, and find it. The Grove is all these things. And more.

What I mean to say is this: the Grove is the location of divine-ly-imagined possibilities where all the elemental stuff, beings, and things of creation coexist in more right relationship with the shared, interconnected being-ness of life, selfhood, one another, and Cre-ator-Spirit. The Sacred Grove is the ever-living, vibrant expression of Creator's infinitely unfolding imagination—the place of endless possibility, human and otherwise, where creation continues unfet-tered and uncontrolled by the dull, homogenized doctrine of like-ness-as-sameness. It is the space into which the Maker of All That Is loves enough to risk releasing a fullness of sacred Potentiality into the cosmos and delights in the ongoing unfolding. It is the place of eternal envisioning where not only are duck-billed platypuses, ax-olotl "walking fish," baobab trees, dragon's blood trees, humming-birds, and pampas grass all manifestations of Holy Imagination, but so too are we gender-transcendent people.

The Sacred Grove is the space into which our Creator breathes, and all that is inhales a life-giving spirit, then exhales the continually shared, cooperative breaths of becoming. It is the space into which God set beginnings and possibilities into creation, looked upon the flourishing and adaptation, and saw it—all of it—was good.

The Sacred Grove is, itself, an Eden-remembrance of sorts *and* the representation of the many tangible spaces in which we come to be who we are. The Grove is the living metaphor for the cosmic *no-thingness* from which we are called into being that, miraculously, becomes the here-and-now, earthly place of our continual becoming the moment we are born into the world.

The Grove is a mystical place, afoot with magic and magical be-coming. It is, also, the very real *and* metaphoric refuge for all who express perpetual in-betweenness, moving in transit through a reso-nate embodied selfhood and the constructs of society and culture. It is the *other-space* where *otherness* is a sacred portion of interdependent unity. It is where all those *made "other"* are *necessary, vibrant particles* of the endlessly-creating divine imagination. This liminal *other-space* is the place of all becoming, where Holy Utterance first spoke, still speaks, and creation comes continually, cooperatively, inter-relationally into being.

It is the timeless, ever-present space where the *Wholly-Other* God sees all that bursts forth from creation, recognizes it is good, and proclaims that goodness. This space is in us, and we are in it. We are images of our Creator's infinite imagining, unleashed into the living world in perpetuity. But we are more still. We, too, are manifestations of God's individuated, relational, connection-seeking likeness and image. We are expressions of our Creator's daring and marvelous *otherness*, flourishing in adaptive, resilient capacities for love, participating fully and creatively in our own ongoing becoming. As surely as God dreamed and imaged the possibility of a platypus, the redwood, and the baobab, God dreamed us as well. And that dream, too, was, is, and ever shall be, good. We are divinely-imaged, uniquely differentiated offspring of Holy Otherness whose continual becoming is visible, notable, and unsettling to the many whose need for orderly, predictable sameness makes them fearful of the magical, trusting, and co-creative trans-formation we embody.

So, we are made *outsider-others* in the constructed world of humanly perceived realities. Where the world of narrow human un-imagining sees and recognizes only two gender possibilities, we recognize, enliven, and embody an infinity of gender potentialities and expressions. Where literalism, limitation, and immutability are prescribed as natural absolutes, we see and understand mutability, multiplicity, fluidity, and thin in-between places. In the binary-minded world where there are only two recognized sexes and any variation is viewed as anomaly or abomination, we know there are innumerable ways for bodies to come into the earthly world, as well as endless imaginaries of forms and functions of bodiedness. It is not merely what we know, but also what we dare to embody that is so troubling to the reductionist, homogenizing antagonists of embodied diversity.

A centuries-old obsession with controlling bodies and selfhood discernments dictates that activities of erotic pleasure and expression must be moderated, controlled, and ultimately should be procreative. But we *other-space dwellers* know that shared erotic attractions and expressions—the consensual communion of bodies intimately connecting, giving, receiving, exploring, discovering, knowing each other—are magical, generatively relational expressions of continual creation, as are our very bodies. We know there is an infinitude of possible affectional, erotic, and sexual attractions and orientations, including celibacy and asexuality, and all of these are equally powerful and transformative ways of being. We understand, in our fleshy personhood, the many ways bodiedness and essence are born and come together in now-ness. We walk in embodied sacred otherness, and sacred otherness walks in us.

Once, in regard for our embodied ways of knowing—our enfleshed-otherness wisdoms—we were set apart as holy people. We were spirit-workers. Healers. Wise people. We were movers between worlds—between grove-worlds and culture-worlds, between *other-space* and *this-space*, between and beyond *being-now* and *becoming*. We were dwellers of barely perceptible transitional, transformative *in-between* spaces, ever present all around and within us. Once, we were shamans, healers, spirit-working wise people. To my mind, in ways equally ancient, contemporary, and arcane, we still are. No doubt, this is why people misunderstand and, so often, fear us. We live and move and have our being in transit through, across, and beyond the world of hive-mind perceptions, beliefs, and permissabilities.

The edge-line boundaries between this *other-space* and the world of human constructs are thin, permeable, like cell membranes; like forest and clearing, river and sea. It is possible, and I am proposing it is so, that we are both, equally, living invitations to notice these *other-space* boundaries, to revere them, and we are, ourselves, invited to embrace and claim our belonging to these vital in-between spaces. We are, I propose, Eden-imaginaries, called to become explorers of a kind—wander-travelers of Sacred Grove-invoking *other-spaces*; excavating, seeking artifacts, discovering and naming the living manifestations of Holy Otherness passing by all around and within us. Everywhere.

Just as the Sacred Grove, itself, testifies to the vibrant bareness of life, we also testify through the miracles of our lives; our mere presence; our survival; our tendencies toward and capacities for thriving. Knowing and embracing this truth, we might feel emboldened to discover other ways to speak what we, in our living on, already proclaim.

We may lift our voices to speak, not only the reality of our living testimonies to the many ways some measure of God's imagining manifests in *otherness*, but to the *necessity* of *other-space dwellers* to a fuller, wider, shared understanding of what it means to be human, who God is (and likely is not), and who we are called to be in a cosmos where God is present. We may engage such declaration-making in pulpits within faith communities where we live and worship. We might find ourselves inclined to step up to podiums and lecterns and speak all manner of holy, liberation-invoking affirmations at town halls, conferences, rallies, or marches. We may even find ourselves compelled to voice the truth of our lives, miracles we have witnessed, and revelations we have discerned, in all kinds of places in between—coffee houses, barber shops, family reunions, neighborhood cookouts, sidewalk cafes. Equally, and just as powerfully, some of us may find the declaration comfortable for us is the miraculous testimony of daring to live on; of showing up for our daily lives, of resisting isolation, venturing out in whatever ways we can and, simply, profoundly, not giving up.

In whatever ways we are able, in the ways of being that work for us, what matters most is this: by the right of our birth into a creation infused with Holy Otherness, we are called to come to know and believe we matter. We are valuable. We are necessary. We are called, I propose, each in our own ways, to notice, affirm, and proclaim the vital necessity of living on. Like the Grove that bears our footprints, living on speaks; sacred syllables burst forth from our daring to be and become ourselves. In the daily miracles of our lives, holy secrets are revealed. We are invited and called, each in our ways of being, to notice, claim, and proclaim the signs of Holiness imaged, present, and discernable in the differentiated particularity in all of creation, entire. Even, and perhaps especially, us.

chapter five

Holy Imaginaries— Incomprehensible and Interconnected

And the Existing One formed the earth-made human from
the dust of the ground and God breathed into their nostrils the
spirit-breath of life; and the human became a living soul ...
Then God took the human and placed them in the garden of Eden,
to settle down, to serve it and to keep it ... And the Holy One said:
"it is not good for the earthling to be alone; I will make a helper to them
conspicuous before them" ... And so, God, the Existing One,
cast a deep sleep upon the earth-made being and they slept; and God
took one of [their] sides and closed the flesh of that place.
Then, the Eternal God fashioned that side God had taken from the
earthling into a partner and brought them to the earth-made being.
Genesis 2:7, 15, 18, 21–22
author's translation

What if we humans were able to reach beyond our own narrow, constructed views of ourselves to hold and develop a more vast, expanded, kaleidoscope-like vision of what constitutes humanity? What
visions of God—and even of ourselves—might we, then, create?
In some practical ways, this question about expanding our view of
humanity underlies all the musings, ponderings, propositions in this
book.

Such a powerful question points to the images and imaginings we, as gender-transcendent people, present to a world bound by artificial, absolutist constructions. It is this power that makes us so frightening to so many. We signify infinite possibility rather than absolutist limitation; we testify to multiplicity and expansiveness; we present, in images of skin and bone and flesh, an endlessly emerging diversity of human beings. Building on the primacy of diversity, our gender-transcendent lives signify that the Creator who fashioned earth-beings in God's own image and likeness *also* created *us*. Indeed, we demonstrate that this Divine Otherness, this Creator-God, had the foresight and intention of creating boundary-busting, threshold-crossing creatures such as us. Such a God divinely ordained our limitless differentiations as images of God's own Divine Imagining. In so many ways, this is at the heart of our proclamation.

Proclamations of Troubling Imagination

As gender-transcendent beings, our bodies, personalities, and ways of being—our particular selves—testify to an entire cosmos of creation too vast, unfettered, and diversity-drenched to be contained. We proclaim a profoundly imaginative Creator. It could be said that the Creator-God infuses God's own particles into every selfhood-endowed being as an act of love and that, in this love, God trusts each and every manifestation of that Holy Imaginary to burst forth into interconnected communion with all that is. In the sacred moments when I begin to fully comprehend these realities proclaimed by our very presence in the world; when I give myself space to simply be held and cradled within the enormity of it all; when I allow myself to dream dreams of the liberating implications our existence offers for all of our human siblings, now and yet to come, I can almost see why our living proclamation is so disorienting for so many people. It is deep and powerful. I can see why, for some, it can be so frightening.

For people who have never been forced against the walls of permissible, but wrongly-fitted personhood, who have never been crushed into narrow, externally imposed identities and, thus, consigned to questioning what it means even to be a self, the images that gender-transcendent people present to the world around us can, indeed, be unsettling. As survivors of various personhood-presses, our presence threatens the neat, orderly worldview that makes earthly beings seem predictable. Moreover, these paradigms of the inexperienced imply that selfhood is static; that life itself is quite stable and, in some way, fixed. Predictable.

And so, faced with implications to the contrary, people are frightened—frightened to allow that the self, let alone the whole of life, is somehow *not* static, that selfhood is both predisposed *and* in flux, to think that selfhood is, at once, stable *and* evolving, to consider that selfhood becomes more fully *self* through continual processes of transformation. We are shaped by pre-existing conditions and external forces, but we are, equally, emergent and unpredictably our own. These realities are especially troubling to people who believe that *who they are* is fixed and that developmental stages are simply an unfolding of narrowly ranging personal variations within a singular, universal form.

We know, through experience, that reaching beyond this reductive mythology requires intentional self-reflection, courageous discernment, and more than a little willingness to be uncomfortable, to be surprised, and to take personal responsibility for being active, co-creative participants in our own becoming. We do not live in a world built upon values and practices congruent with becoming an authentic person. We do not live in a world that encourages us to claim a sense of personhood rooted in holy potentialities and endless possibilities. By boldly living on, we proclaim. We proclaim such becoming as part of the nature of things. Yet, we live in a world that fears recognizing and working through the tender, mysteriously revealing ambiguities, paradoxes, and complexities needful to discerning selfhood and becoming a person.

And so, we are always making our way through lands not made for us, places not suited to sustain us, and environments inhospitable and unaccommodating to our needs—let alone our hopes, dreams, gifts, and contributions. We are always moving in transit between and across the spaces in-between—the borderland, threshold spaces between who we actually are and who we are presumed to be, who we know ourselves to be and who we are allowed to be, and, especially, who we have been and who we are always becoming. Ever in search of flourishing beyond mere survival, we are positioned in ways that necessitate finding, or indeed creating for ourselves, spaces in which we can—with some measure of security, sustaining shelter, and affirmation—be fully and expressively who we are. In this way, we are beings born of the cosmic, Eden-like Sacred Grove who are, also, boundary-betrayers, edge-walkers, liminal beings caught between two worlds.

We are thrust from the womb of the Sacred Imaginary, the Divine Imagination, into a world of unimagining, built on ideas and images of constriction and control. We are born into constructed absolutes and reductive ideologies. Ways of being are prescribed for us—ways that they claim originated with the Creator. The makers of such ideologies ground their position in the Creation and assert natural laws that are congruent with *their* interpretation of the Genesis stories—while simultaneously unmaking the God of Creation into their own self-referencing image and likeness.

Expressing God's Image

The working construct of God in so many of our sacred stories (particularly those shared between Jewish and Christian traditions) is actually made in the image of certain, particular humans. The God who made all humans in God's own image and similitude is continually re-made, over and over, into the dramatically more limited image of ruling class men. Not only that, these unmakers of God hold fast to ideas about "humanity" that are expressly and intentionally crafted into a conglomerate image of themselves as if this image is fixed in nature and, therefore, universal.

The fancy word for this is *anthropomorphizing*: human beings *creating God* in the image and likeness of humans. Ultimately, this is only natural because we, being not-God, can never fully apprehend or comprehend that which is God. We can only apprehend what we *perceive*, and *receive*, as our experiences of God—and we comprehend those experiences within the frameworks offered by our mundane experiences in these bodies, in these lives, in this world and all its contexts. This, in fact, is what our scripture-writing ancestors were doing. They were not seeking, so much, to prove the *existence* of God as to convey their *sense of God* in a world—a cultural context—in which the existence of God (or many gods) was *assumed.* Our ancestors were communicating with each other, thus leaving for all who came after them, their individual and communal understanding of God, who God is, and how God acts in relationship to, and with, the whole of creation. They used their languages, and their images, to tell of their experiential understanding of a strangely relational, yet transcendent God. They gave each other—and us—not God, God-self, but their stories about God.

All of our language for describing God is, by nature and function, inadequate. And, all our language for God is ultimately analogical—comparative images, descriptive metaphors, and similes that can never fully capture or apprehend their subject because the subject is, quite simply, beyond us. God, the subject of all our imaginative and linguistic striving, is by nature incomprehensible in God's fullness. All we have, ultimately, are our perceptions and our experiences. Often, though not always, like Jacob (Genesis 28:16), we see in retrospect. Our inability to fully apprehend this being we call God is, I believe, as it should be. If God were to be something we could comprehend entirely, that we could fully capture in intellect and reason, such a being would no longer be that which is God; it would become, completely, something else—indeed, something smaller and much less interesting.

The same could be said of our language not only for gender but also for descriptions of any human being. Our descriptive language is at once necessary and also inadequate. For it can never fully capture or apprehend its subject. This is no coincidence. Each human being is an enspirited, embodied, ever-becoming person made in the image of this incomprehensible Divine Otherness. We are, each one, knowable only through relationship, through bearing witness, and through interactive experience. As above, so below: God and each of us are knowable only through encounter, through our experiences, sensations, and perceptions.

Something magical happens when we allow ourselves to move beyond boring ideas of God to embrace a kaleidoscopic God who is as diverse as the humanity we have witnessed before our very eyes. By taking a wider view of humanity, we also take a wider view of God.

Enspirited, Spiritual Beings

One of the primary creation stories about God and us, as earth-bound beings, is given to us in a foundational creation story in Genesis 2. The text tells us that God formed the first human from the dust of the ground, then breathed the breath of life—*nishmat chayim*—into the human's nostrils, and they became a living being. This *breath of life* is some measure of God's own spirit. It is the moment, so the story goes, when human beings become *enspirited*—that is, this is the first exhalation of God's self, God's soul, into the whole of humanity, giving us each a soul: the spirit-breath which, then, through the miracles of our continuing emergence into the world, is passed through and among us, shared between us, and enlivens us all. This means that we are, by nature and birth, spiritual beings. Moreover, we are all, each and every one of us, endowed with, filled, and animated by the living Spirit of God.

It could be said that, in our daring to live-on, to insistently exist and persist, our presence proclaims and expresses the creative, interconnective Spirit of God. I am proposing that this is, in some mysterious way, true. Much to the discomfort of those who believe gender-transcendent persons are abominations, I am asserting that we, as gender-transcendent persons, are uniquely essential embodiments of unfettered Divine Spirit. This enspirited condition, this soul-breath, is what it means to spiritual beings by nature—that is, to be breath-invigorated, en-souled beings. Meanwhile, this spiritual nature is also the fundamental common characteristic of what it means to be a human being. Further, this enspirited condition makes us all, in some measure, just a little bit divine—even, and perhaps, especially, gender-transcendent persons because we dare to live from and through the spirit within us. That is, we are compelled by it, guided into fuller and fuller selfhood, and empowered to resist all manner of dull, unimaginative prescriptions of what it means to be a person.

I am further proposing that we, especially, speak vibrant testimonies to the reality that to be a human being is to be an enspirited being. This spiritual nature is more than we have been conditioned to believe. It has nothing to do with the tenets of religion and everything to do with the core aspects of what it is to be a living, breathing, daring, and dreaming human being. We are in fact, not made spiritual *by* religion. Religion is made to exist because we are, by nature, spiritual beings.

That is: to be a human being is to be endowed with the spirit-breath of identity, of selfhood, the primary characteristic of which is a capacity for, and disposition toward, vital, marvelously complex, and interrelated states of longing—not only for the means of a life, such as shelter, food, and basic resources, but also for place, belonging, community, and some sense of purpose and contribution to something beyond ourselves. Deeper still are longings for loving and being loved, for intimacy, for family of some sort, and most especially, for being seen, regarded, and understood by others whom we also seek to know. Fundamentally, we long for the space and resources to engage in becoming an actualized, authentic, and flourishing person in active relationship with the world around us. Along with these most basic yearnings are longings for various forms of happiness, for creative expression, for meaning-making, for all manner of knowledge, discovery, and truth-seeking, for self-expression, dreaming and imagining, and for an infinite array of other desires, hopes, and hungers. To be a person is to be enspirited with identity, endowed with various states of longing.

It is possible that this enspirited disposition, this capacity for longing, is the single most vital thing we, as human beings, share in common. Perhaps, it is also, in some measure, what it means to be living expressions of God's image and likeness—perhaps, especially for gender-transcendent persons, we whose longing is so deep, whose yearnings for actualizing our self-understanding, for self-expression, happiness, even for the most basic elements of survival, are met with so much resistance and subjugation. I propose that our capacities for daring existence, to preserve and express multiple and complex states of longing are, at least, one way that we reflect God's image.

Creating Relationship

Not only are we reflections of God's Image and Imagination. I am further proposing that the creative movements within our sacred stories in Genesis 1 and 2 show us a Creator-God who is actually not the Maker of rigid binary genders and predictable sexualities as the fearful extremists want to believe. Of course, God *did*—we are told—make binaries. Indeed, binaries exist as surely as I live and breathe. However, I assert that the God of Images and Imagination *imaged* and *imagined* us as well. God is the Creator and Ordainer of diversely-manifesting persons who *transcend those very same binaries*. Indeed, I want to argue that this Creator-God is the Designer of relationality itself—and that such relationality is part of what makes humanity sacred, divinely imaged, if not actually divine.

All of this is inextricably connected. In Genesis 2, we find that the text our ancestors left for us is quite explicit in this regard, despite eons of misdirected readings that deform a more direct and plain reading of the text. Indeed, the whole project of creation implies that the Creator seeks, always, relationship with each one of us individually and with all of creation more broadly. So, let us start from the beginning again.

All that *is*, every *thing* God has called into being, and every being formed from the ground, we are told, came into being through, and was made to exist within, interconnected relationship. The waters above and the waters below were connected in relationship. The land and the waters were joined together by relational connections. So, too, were the creatures made to live upon the land, in the air, and in the seas, rivers, and streams. All the vegetation lived in relationship with everything that was. And, then, God created the being made from the dust of the ground.

In Hebrew, *ha-adam* means "the adam," the person made from the ground. The language itself connects this first human to the earth. The *ha-adam*, the first human, was made from the *ha-adamah*, meaning "the ground." The first human was not only made of moistened, dusty earth, but shares substance, indeed identity, with the earth.

As the Creator formed the various creatures and presented them to that first earth-being to name and to care for, God realized that the human was, ultimately, alone; there was, in all of creation, no similar being available to be a help to this newly-formed person. And so, in a moment of miraculously responsive relationship, this Unknowable Creator God realized that it was not good for the human being to be alone. That is, God realized this undifferentiated, presumably self-contained, self-sufficient human being needed *more.* At minimum, the earth-being needed what the animals and creatures had: another being, similar to, but not the same as themself; a partner-companion differentiated from, but compatible with them. Beyond relationships to the earth and the many creatures of land, air, and waters, the original human being, it seems, needed a *human relationship.*

In this story, we find an involved, caring Creator who realized independent, extraordinary self-sufficiency was not sufficient to this new world and way of *being* that God had just set into ever-evolving motion. God's hopes and dreams for the human being were more than a life of lonely, solitary singularity. This Creator-God understood that any person left solely to their own company and self-reliance is destined to unhappiness, fundamentally disconnected from all the plentiful, expansive life—and lives—present and abundant all around them. Such a person, alone and disconnected, will inevitably become a believer in their own primacy and supremacy. Indeed, if I am all that matters, then what else is there? Such a person becomes the center of their own grandiose universe, believing that they were created for and exist for their own purpose alone.

Such a person is fundamentally disconnected from any and all things larger and more vast than them—the natural world, their community, neighboring communities, and even, perhaps, God. A person left alone and so disconnected may become despondent and disconsolate, or they may become arrogant and self-absorbed. Yet, God created in us an inner sea of unmet longing, so that we might not be left to suffer such a fate of despondency and despair. God understood what humans frequently fail to comprehend: if trees and plants, birds and water-creatures, animals and insects, all need the company and community of distinct, individual others like themselves, then so, too, do we humans.

And so, God differentiated the earth-being, not for the creation of gender, in and of itself, but expressly for the purpose of bringing into creation a particular kind of relationship—a distinctly human relationship, characterized by mutual need and support, by shared qualities and attributes and capabilities, and by enough likeness and difference to make for each other compatible partners. This relationality forms a kind of covenant, an engaged mutuality and reciprocity of relational interdependence with one another, as well as with the garden-land, with nature, and with the Creator God who gave us, one to another. It could be said that God surmised humans would, first, need to learn about being in relationships with one another to be in some form of relationship with God's own intangible being, with God's otherness.

Divine Surgery

So, God, the Cosmic Surgeon, caused a deep sleep to come over that first human, anesthetizing the earth-being, lovingly protecting this tender person from both the immediate pain of isolation and the pending separation. Then, God separated the earth-person at the side, carefully closed up the earth-being's wound, and formed a new helper-companion. When God finished forming these two intimately bound, yet separate, persons, God brought them together into garden-dwelling relationships—with one another, with the garden, with vegetation, with an abundance of earth creatures, and with their Creator.

In Hebrew, the word normally translated as "rib," is important; it does not actually mean rib, specifically. The Hebrew word is *tsela*, and it primarily means, simply, "side." It is also a word profoundly pertinent to Trans-Forming Proclamation. The word, *tsela*, is not used abundantly in the Hebrew canon. But, when it is used, the subjects are significant. Most often, the word is employed to describe the construction of holy things—namely, the Ark of the Covenant, the Tabernacle tent that accompanied the people in the wilderness, and then later, the Holy Temple. Thus, it can be said, these earth-creatures God formed were also holy habitations born in the Creator's imagination, formed from the ground of Creator's sacred earth, brought forth in profound relational connection to the earth, to each other, and to God.

These relational states are essential to God's visions for the project of creation. In fact, the rabbinic sages say that humans were not formed from just any old patches of earth, but were formed from moistened dirt taken from the four corners of the earth (Midrash Tanchuma Pekudei 3:16). This God did so that, wherever a person goes, the earth will not reject them. Indeed, if even the ground from which we come is meant to welcome us, how much more so should the peoples of the lands welcome one another?

And so, it was: God created multiple, interconnected relationships within God's good creation. A key feature of this relationality is that likeness does *not* mean sameness. Human beings are made in some likeness, some similitude, to God; but humans most decidedly are *not* God. And so, to create a meaningful and significant capacity for various forms of relatability between human beings, we, too, need to be differentiated, distinct persons. Mirroring our *likeness* to Holy-Otherness, we are *like* but needfully *other-than* one another, much as we are other from God.

This reality, the idea of being similar but not the same, is made notable by the use of a specific Hebrew word. The word in Genesis 2:18, variously translated as "suitable to him" or "compatible to him" or even "corresponding to him," with regard to Eve, is taken from the root word *neged*. *Neged* most appreciably means "that which is conspicuous," or "what is straightforward, in front of, or opposite of something or someone." The being we come to know as Eve was compatible or suitable to the post-surgical Adam, as a help-mate, *precisely* because of Eve's *conspicuousness*—that is, because Eve was *noticeably different* from Adam, set apart, and distinct. The newly separated and transformed Adam and Eve were differentiated from one another by unique, particular, and distinct identities and personalities. They were individuated, yet each was a part of the other, not unlike the measure of God's own breath within them. This, so it seems, is the relationality Creator-God made—a species-bound similarity, expressed in diverse, individual particularity, invigorated with a portion of God's own Spirit, and interdependently connected to all that is.

In the project of Trans-Forming Proclamation, I propose that the disposition toward innate individuality both creates *and* is necessary for fulfilling our relational capacities. In other words, our being unique individuals makes possible—and is needful to—our capacity for *communal connection*. The remedy to humanity's original, independent self-reliance and self-sufficiency occurred when our ancestors were separated into distinct, separate beings—distinct both from the earth and its creaturely inhabitants, but connected; part of, and connected to, each other, but also differentiated *from one another.*

Our relationality shapes and forms who we are as individual persons. We were both created and born into relational communities disposed to synergistic interdependence. Said another way, there is, really, no such thing as completely independent or fully self-made persons—certainly, not since the original *adam.* All of us are who we are *because* others *are*, also, and because of how they have been, and are, in relationship with us. We are in the world together and made from the same cosmic stuff; that connectivity is a part of us, arguably passed down to us from that original sacred surgery. We always carry something of one another with us—as surely as we breathe, thereby invigorating the Holy Breath within us, just as surely as we inhabit bodies composed of the earthly elements that connect us to all that is.

I am fully aware that some insist Eve was created *from* Adam—from, even, a presumably expendable or surplus body part, a rib. Such persons go on to derive from that premise all manner of constrictive and oppressive directives about people who are women, about androcentric male primacy, and about gender and sexuality. To adopt such views is not only to miss the inherent equality of those newly-formed first humans, but it is also to miss one of the most beautiful and significant truths offered in these storied images.

The *adam* was one expression of personhood before *the divine surgery* out of which the being, Eve, was made. But, the original *adam*—the first earth-made human—was changed, transformed, to become a different, differentiated, and distinct person. Prior to the sacred separation, the *adam* was not a relational being in the way that the post-surgical being we call Adam would become. The story is clear: "the" *adam* became Adam; thus, Adam is a unique individual person because of Eve, just as Eve is a unique individual person because of Adam. If Eve was "made from" a part of Adam, then, too, Adam was "made from" the leftovers of Eve. In a sense, Adam came more fully to life when Eve came to life.

The person, who in English is called Eve, in Genesis 3:20, is actually named for this relational miracle. Her given name is *Chavah*, which is a causative form and derives from the Hebrew word for "life." Thus, *Chavah* means "one who *causes* others to live." Moreover, our capacities for relational connection are, in a profoundly allegorical way, name-giving. That is, being in relationship with one another provides experiential foundations through which we perceive, receive, and come to know one another. Through their relationship, Adam discerned language, words, to describe his experiential understanding of who she was to and with him—and all who came after her. In other words, the name he offered had been discerned through their life together in this new world. More simply put, Adam discerned she was a "life-giver." Following this, I propose that our relational nature, itself, is actually life-giving.

Indeed, because of Eve, all of us—including what remains of the original *adam*—are given life. Because Eve came into being, humanity became a web of relationally connected beings, distinct from and unique to one another. Our capacity for various types of relationships contributes to who we are and, equally, depends upon our unique individuality. The two attributes of individuality and community are intimately bound and inseparable.

Authenticity in Relationship

Moreover, these insights call us to deepen our understanding of the many ways that we move within and express our relational nature. But also, we might come to better understand how our distinctions affect, or determine, whether our relationships are life-giving or life-diminishing—or, worse, life-taking. What I mean to say is this: when others fail to recognize and accept our sense of self; when others interact, speak, and relate with us in ways that diminish our personhood; when others behave toward us in ways that disregard our self-understanding; when others fail to reflect back to us who we present ourselves to be, they take from us, measure by life-diminishing measure, the essential relational exchanges, acceptances, and affirmations needful to being, and continuing to become, an authentic, self-actualizing, and developing person.

When we are misnamed, we are diminished. When our selfhood is ignored, something vital is taken from us. Equally, when any person meets and engages a person in ways that confirm, affirm, and demonstrate recognition of them, some measure of life is given to them. This is especially true for us as gender-transcendent persons. None of us, from our common ancestors onward, is an island—and even islands are in relationship to the waters around them. Nor are we identical to one another. We are who we are because others *are*, because they are *not-us*, and especially, because we are *formed* in relational communities *with them*.

From a Trans-Forming Proclamation point of view, it could be said that, often, for a person to become an authentic self, to align fully with that internal sense of self that goes with us from that Sacred Grove, an individual's entire way of being and way of being received may need to undergo trans-formation. Such a trans-formation strengthens one's sense of self, which then—and only then—makes them more able to be in authentic relationships with others, including and perhaps especially, God. Said more plainly—that is, to make a Trans-Forming Proclamation—since I made changes in how I present to others, chose a name that fits me, made alterations to my body that make it more livable for me, and claimed a way of being in the world that more congruently projects who I understand myself to be, I am more fully who I am. It is precisely because of these changes that I am more fully able to be in authentic relationships with others and the world around me. I am deeply aware that this is true for others as well.

Thus, the more we become authentically who it is in us to be, the more able we are to be in genuine relationships with others—and the more we fulfill God's plan for our humanity: that we, creatures of spirit, bone, and earth, should not be alone.

Moreover, *both* Adam *and* Eve came *more fully into being* in that moment of sacred relationship-making cosmic surgery. As it often is with human relationships, neither of them was the same after that first encounter. *Both* of them were changed and transformed. Authentic selfhood, experienced and expressed in genuine, open, and mutually affirming relationships, changes us. It shapes us. It leaves a mark. Indeed, even difficult or problematic relationships leave a mark.

When relationships are forgotten, neglected, or, especially, misused, relationships can diminish and harm who we are. When relationships are reciprocal, mutually encouraging, and affirming, we become more fully ourselves within them. Conversely, the less mutually regarding and beneficial our relationships are, the less able we are to be and become ourselves. It is possible, I would argue, that the more we are willing to be changed through our being in the world of others, the more fully ourselves we become—and, thus, the more fully human we become.

Relationships matter because *all* relationships—between land and water, between cities and groves, between human beings, and between God and creation—*are* matter. It is clear that God, the Relational One, created and ordained relationality as a life-giving and life-affirming component of what it is to be a human person. More pointedly, experiences of being seen for who we are by others are essential to being and becoming a congruent, authentic self. This means having our self reflected back to us through others, as well as finding growth and continued development in and through mutually-engaged, reciprocal relationships with others. Healthy relational connections contribute to our ongoing, evolutional becoming. Therefore, as essential as others are to us, we are also essential to others. Our individuality is not in opposition to our relationality. It is intimately connected to this inherent capacity. Relationality is, essentially, the means through which our individuality is expressed and becomes both accessible and meaningful.

Breaking Open the Binary

Centuries of incurious and reductive readings have taught us to take the dominant distillations of these stories for granted—to assume and accept that traditional readings are *the* intended, definitive, and *only* readings. This approach is particularly common within Christendom. Figuratively speaking, we have been conditioned to move unconsciously through the garden of our beginnings while being directed to miss *both* the forest and the wood. We have somehow been taught to look away from the trees altogether. But the forest and the wood speak our embodied languages of relationality.

Still, there are those who actively balk at such magnificent revelations. Some readers need to confine humanity within well-ordered boxes. Thus, eons of gender (and sexuality) reductive readings have also pointed to the verse in Genesis 1:27, which is commonly read to say: "God created 'man' in *His* own image, in the image of God, *He* created him; *male* and *female* He created them" (emphases added, author's translation). Doubtless there is a lot in this single verse that could be picked apart. For now, I want to focus on what I believe to be the primary misreadings at work in reductionist interpretations. To read Genesis 1 (or any of the scriptures, really) as a historical record or a detailed description of a presumed historical event, is to fundamentally misread not only the verse, but the entire chapter.

Genesis 1, like other sections of Hebrew scripture, is intentionally-crafted, high literature. It is a poem—a rather lovely and thoughtfully worded one at that. It employs poetic literary tropes and devices commonly accepted as good writing for hundreds and hundreds of years since. An especially fine example is the repetition of the phrase, "and there was evening and there was morning" a succession of six days.

Although literary criticism is not my primary point, this is relevant to understanding the particular "clobber" verse at which we are looking. The phrase "male and female" can be read as a particular rhetorical device consistent with the other poetic tropes in the text. Specifically, it can be read as a "merism." A "merism" is "a form of rhetorical synecdoche," which means contrasting parts or representatives of a whole are used to refer to or describe an entire thing, image, or concept (merriam-webster.com). For example, it is common to use the phrase "young and old" to describe a group of people consisting not only of young and aging people, but also everyone in between—with all ages present and represented by juxtaposing the poles of a range. Thus, "male and female" can be taken to mean men, women, and every gender between or beyond those two end points. God created not *only* males and females, but a whole host of variously gendered, individuated human beings who manifest diversely differentiated sexes, sexualities, and gender identities.

Moreover, the reductive reading glosses over the glaring reality later repeated in Genesis 2. The word *adam* is not a proper name. It is a word that, as I have described previously, means *being from the ground*, the *adamah*. It is, simply, a noun. This is made obvious in the Hebrew by the fact that the term, *adam*, is phrased repeatedly with the Hebrew definite article, *ha*, so it reads *ha-adam*, and means *the adam*. The term refers to a specific, proto-human made from the stuff of the whole earth, who became relational and more fully a person by being trans-formed into a conspicuously individual person.

Meanwhile, Hebrew is a gendered language (like French or Spanish, for example), which means some words are gendered feminine and others are gendered masculine. It is a feature of the language, not biology. So, *the adam* is presumed to be male because the word, *adam*, does not possess a feminine suffix, whereas, *adamah*—the earthy ground—is feminine because it carries the feminine suffix, *ah*. As another noun, *adamah*, too, is prefixed with the definite article, and appears as *ha-adamah*, which is to say *"the" earthy ground*. Based upon the context of the story, itself, and the gendered nature of Hebrew, *adam*, comes to mean "mankind," or "humankind/humanity," in addition to functioning, post-sacred-surgery, as a proper noun, or name.

Moreover, in these texts, the statement that some things exist (such as males and females) *never* implies other things *do not exist.* It is a logic error to suggest otherwise. The text never says that people we now describe as intersex, agender, non-binary, or gender- transcendent do not—or *cannot*—exist as natural manifestations of humanity arising. In fact, there are plenty of places where gender-transcendent characters come to life in sacred text, such as some thirty-eight examples of eunuchs in the Hebrew scriptures—all of whom, as the stories go, played important roles in doing God's work in the earthly realm.

Doubtless, our ancestors also understood there are many ways to come into being, to be born, just as there are many ways to be intimately relational with others. I am proposing that, regardless of how we read these two stories, God's vastly ranging relational capacities, and God's decision to imbue human beings with some similitude of those same relational capacities, *are emphatic.* Moreover, both Genesis 1 and 2 are stories born within our ancestors' profound experiences of something moving, relationally, in their lives which they perceived to be God. Those experiences shaped how they understood their God, just as their cultural contexts shaped how they crafted and employed thoughtful poetics and other literary tropes throughout the biblical texts.

Both Genesis 1 and 2 make use of binary merisms to describe a range of possibilities, potentialities, and even persistent mysteries inherent in all of creation, including—and especially—human beings. These literary tropes are stunning in their layered implications of interconnected relationality: waters above and waters below; waters and land masses; evening and morning; Adam and Chavah (Eve). Additionally, these stories do not propose to be historical narrative in the ways that we, in our contexts, conceive of details we presume to be historical facts. Rather, these stories are the spiritual histories of a particular people, in particular times, growing and developing into a particular peoplehood with each other, the world around them, and their God. The Genesis stories, especially, lay the initial foundation of this spiritual history and its rootedness in relationality as both a characteristic of the Creator-God, of creation itself, and of human beings. Sadly, the manipulation of these stories has laid foundational excuses for an array of persecutions and oppressions that simply are not confirmed by the stories themselves.

From another literary viewpoint, we could also say that the one who is assigned status as male (in this case Adam) and the one who is assigned female status (in this case Eve) are, on one level, accidents of gendered suffixes and the details of Hebrew linguistics/semantics. However, it is also fundamentally true—and *more important* to remember—that the sociocultural ideas constructed around maleness and femaleness, femininity and masculinity, were *previously established* in the social mindset of the culture and, therefore, present in the formation of linguistic communication. These gendered ideas were in place long before the language evolved to the forms fixed by the Hebrew scriptures and even longer before the scriptures themselves were transcribed from oral tradition to written words.

In truth, we are always reading scripture—and, really, any text—*backward*. That is, from where we are, from our contexts, assumptions, and biases, we are reading our way through an existing text, trying to sort out contexts far removed from our own and hoping to find meaning and insights relevant to our lives. In doing so, it can be easy to forget that these texts—and indeed, all written texts—are also *written backwards*. Said another way, our ancestors had significant, meaning-bearing experiences so profound that those experiences inspired stories. These became part of their orally transmitted traditions, and later, they wrote them down. The stories were not written as they were unfolding, but later, after many tellings, reflections, continuing interpretations, and deeper meaning-making, even as they continued to experience this Force-Presence they called God.

In fact, we do the same thing. We seek to make meaning of our experiences and the whole of our lives. We speak, write, make art, dance, sing songs, and tell our stories. Sometimes, those stories are about who we understand ourselves to be, who we believe we are becoming, and sometimes, who we discern God might be. Or not, as the case may be for some of us. The stories are not, in fact, the events or experiences. This book is an example—one example among many—and only one example of my own writing through thinking about what it is to be a person, who I experience Holy Otherness to be, and how I experience the world of others. Our ancestors were telling the stories that developed in their search for sense of self, peoplehood, and God—as well as justice and right conduct. These are the stories they felt important enough to pass on from generation to generation.

Scripturally, all this is pretty mind-bending and heady stuff to wrap thoughts around, though on one level the details may seem small. Ultimately, all these layers of meaning and implications arise within the gendered, highly descriptive, metaphoric, and allegorical language of Hebrew and in the time-bound context of our ancestors' understanding of creation; who we humans are, as people; who God is (or is not); and how all these elements are, or might be, connected. Their stories, describing and exploring these understandings, are first and foremost, literature.

Through biased, reductive interpretations, these texts have been transformed into uninteresting, dull prescriptions about gender and cisgender-heterosexual sex. However, we find more rich and spiritually expansive meanings when these stories are read as the high literature that they are, motivated and informed, both by the assumption that God exists and by impactful experiences of this Sacred Presence. To glean deeper, less oppressive, more spiritually liberating meanings, we are helped by reading and understanding these stories as imaginative, creative stories—even spiritual history—rather than scientific command.

Holy Imaginaries, Divine Imagination

These are the truth-laden thought-worlds of our ancestors, infused with marvelous personhood-affirming and humanity-expanding, earth-grounding images and proclamations. The sad thing is that the makers of institutions, containers of God, and keepers of power, fearful of natural diversity, have manipulated them through the ages—because, to be truthful, creating God-fearing narratives is a powerful tool for creating compliance in people. Still, these are the stunning poetics of a spiritual, rather than reductionist, history that has been weaponized into active proscriptions against any expressions of gender, sex, or sexuality that contradict the constructed norms of our dominant-dominating culture. By minimizing humanity—and God—reductive literalism produced classifications morphed into ideological weapons that serve to marginalize diverse, expansive expressions of gender identities.

Beginning at the beginning reminds us that, as the stories go, the place into which we were created was, in fact, a grove. Genesis 1 and 2, differently, each through a specific voice, describe a significant image: *the grove came first.* Before us, there was already a place. Into that place, God-made beings were created to live in harmonious mutuality with the lands, the seas, the skies, and one another. The theological point is large and unmistakable. Our Creator so longed for opportunities to engage in multiple, interactive relational experiences that God transformed God's own longing into an energetic, vibratory moment of creative yearning. God sighed. And, in that longing exhalation, God uttered the holy words that called forth the light into the void, between the waters above and the waters below the expanse, within a formless cosmos.

Light burst forth into the darkness. And, our Creator saw that the light was good. Then, God spoke, and the great luminaries came into being to fill the nighttime and the daytime—and the spectral relationship between light and darkness began. God uttered words filled with atoms, elements, and compounds and all the rich vegetation, fruit-bearing trees, seed-yielding plants, flowers, sheltering trees, and bushes necessary for a wide and sustaining grove came into being upon all the earth. With light to nurture growth and darkness to offer rest, our Creator separated the lands from the seas and brought forth all the multitudes of diverse creatures to fill the earth, sky, and waters. Then, with luminaries, sustenance, and shelter in place, Creator-God fashioned humans from the ground of the earth, formed earthly creatures to accompany them, and set them all to live, and move, and have their being in the garden. And God saw that it was, all of it, good.

All of this God did, it seems, not only to provide us with life-sustaining plants, sources of food and shelter, and creatures to help and to accompany us, but, first and foremost, God did this to give us a sense of *place*. For as much as earth-beings need food, shelter, and resources, human beings need a place to call home—a place to live and grow, work and dream, together, on a patch of ground that will never reject us. We come from the Sacred Grove, we belong to it, and this earth-grove is part of us. We, as living, breathing earth-bound beings, need a real, tangible sense of belonging—a home in body *and* in world, a physical space in which to live and move, to grow and to dream, to be and become, and especially, to interact with and relate to one another. God put us in such a place—in a Sacred Grove— filled with community, with communal mutuality. We were not only placed into, but born of this sanctuary, this protected place—where we are surrounded by kindred souls who are similar but not the same, woven together in an ever-threading, ever-weaving living loom of becoming in which we are, each of us, miraculously, both thread and co-creative weaver. It has been called Eden, this place of our ancestral emergence. It is the place where we become fully ourselves, uniquely woven into this verdant, living web of interdependence.

We were given such a world because the Ever-Relational Holy Other came to understand that we need relational connection to our world, and especially, to conspicuous others who are yet similar to ourselves. We need these interdependent relational reciprocities in order to learn how to be more fully who we are, individually and collectively—including but not limited to our relationship with God. Yet, this interrelational world, composed of interconnected particles and elements, beings and life-ways, has become rather lost to us as we have moved farther and farther away from Eden. In leaving the germinal sanctuary Grove, our human community has become tangled and choked, like an untended, forgotten garden full of weeds. Amid the constructed worlds of human unimagining, we have lost our collective capacity to apprehend our Creator's endlessly-unfolding, living imaginary of miraculous, marvelously particular beings. The Sacred Grove has been, with greater and greater intent and sophistication, effectively replaced with colonialist, occupier-settler, empire building.

Empires serve the powerful who create them. And, empires rely upon the labor and loyalty of bodies put to work to build and maintain them. Empires require constrictive systems, structures, and institutions that serve to lift up and lionize the nation state and its leaders—and, more importantly, to contain and control the very people on whose lives and labor the empire is built. As such, the makers of empire cannot maintain power and dominance if the people go around freely re-imagining themselves and live-dreaming dreams of Eden. Thus, the earth-bound Divine Imaginary, through intention and effort, becomes reduced, minimized, and reshaped into the images and narratives suitable to, and supportive of, the imperialist culture.

Into this world of human unimagining, this constructed perversion of our Creator's intent, we gender-transcendent persons emerge, generation after generation, to help us remember. This we do despite all the many various and combined efforts to wish us away, to erase us, and to assure our demise in a world of intentional, unoriginal constructed permissibilities of personhood. And, in our continual emerging, in our daring to exist, to live on, we make profound proclamations from the eternal, grove-ground of the still-living Divine Imaginary.

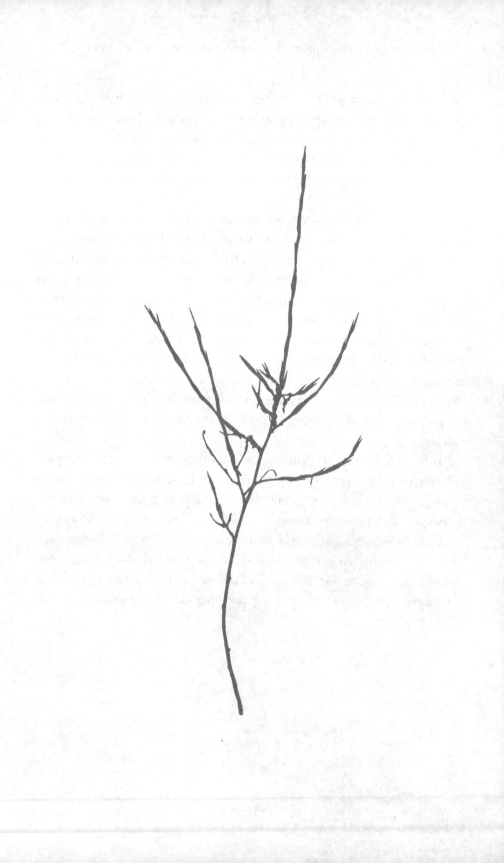

chapter six

Shedding Skin

Then Joshua rose early in the morning;
and he and all the sons of Israel set out from
Shittim and came to the Jordan,
and they lodged there before they crossed.
Joshua 3:1
New American Standard translation

The Grove is liminal. [It] exists just over the threshold-space
we step lightly and decidedly across, one foot on the firm fecund
ground, the other in the equally embodied, equally sensual,
inexplicably transcendent other-space of gender-transcendent presence.
And, there, we remember: these are inseparable.
Excerpt, Chapter Four: Sacred Grove, Living Proclamation

On any given transition from the crowded populace to clusters of forests and groves, it is quite possible to happen upon an apparently list-
less snake, slightly hidden within a scattering of fallen leaves, under
the cover of a random collection of rocks, or nestled within a pile of
fallen limbs and branches. Quietly leaning in for a closer look might
also reveal tell-tale indications that the snake is preparing to shed its
skin—bluish, milky film over the eyes; obvious lethargy; dull color-
ing of the scales.

During the process, the reptile secretes the milky substance between the old and the new layers of skin that makes shedding possible. The snake is in a highly vulnerable state during this time. In fact,

61

it is partially, if not completely, sightless as it prepares to shed. In the natural world, inability to see a predator is deadly. For this reason, snakes seek refuge as they prepare to shed their confining skin and loose themselves from restrictions that hinder their continued growth.

In this way, snakes are our skin-shedding kindred. We know what the snake knows: becoming who we are means engaging the work of vulnerability. It means breaking open the outgrown, constricting skin and stretching through it. Becoming means pushing against abrasive surfaces to reveal what is hidden—rubbing along surrounding rocks, the bark of trees, coarse clumps of grass, and pressing, wriggling, tugging, and pulling free from all that binds the self within. The snake knows what we also know experientially: growing means shedding skin, repeatedly. Over and over, again.

I learned this lesson from my grandmother when I was young. Something within my younger self that I could not yet name understood this knowledge was significant—that it was magical wisdom; that it would, at some point, hold meaning for my own life. Most of the important lessons I've learned, those from Sacred Grove and everyday world alike, have been like this: wisdoms seen only dimly, made clear, meaningful, and truth-bearing over time and through personal experience. Many of these early lessons came to me from my maternal grandmother.

Throughout my formative years, Grandmother Daught (short for "daughter" in my great grandfather's vernacular) taught me many things. From the day I was born, she sang hymns to me, told me stories, offered up aphorisms and allegories, and called me into the learning-labs of her kitchen, gardens, and surrounding history-laden grounds and streams. She also encouraged me to follow my grandfather around where I learned about cursing, repairing things, the basics of carpentry, and the value of silence. As I grew, I realized she was teaching me more than how to do things like make tasty pies, plant flowering and fruit-bearing things, or identify things like bird species, fossils, arrow heads, pieces of old pottery, geodes, various minerals, and gemstones—though all of that was good. To this day,

I am still a rock, gem, fossil, archeology, and nature-revering geek. It is just part of who I am—this seeking out and carrying with me all sorts of earth-borne treasures.

The point is, Grandmother was teaching me a life-way: she was passing down wisdoms, insights, and lessons about life and living that she had gleaned from her own experience and from the Scottish-Creek Indian (Muscogee) Grove-born wisdom and knowledge-way traditions passed on to her. Looking back through my memories with more attentive vision and perspectives, I wish I remembered more than I do. Grandmother was not only a wisdom and memory keeper of a kind; she was also a teacher of all sorts of mystical, magical things.

Through the natural world, Grandmother Daught taught me about life, human nature, and especially our relationships to creation and Creator. She passed on to me her Creator God. Her God was the Crafter of cosmic relationality and interdependence; her God was the Former of the fecund earth and all that walks, crawls, slithers, hops, jumps, and creeps upon it; her God set in motion all that flies, swarms, and glides above the earth, as well as all that swims and grows in its fresh and salty waters, marsh lands, swamps, and bogs. Grandmother's God is the Indwelling Creator of all that is, Maker of black-capped chickadees, irises, crickets, peep frogs, and even each of us. Her God, Keeper of our tender lives, is my God, too—the Sustainer, who accompanied me when the days were deeply dark and nearly endless; when the tense, fragile line between self-loathing and daring self-love seemed unbearable; when it felt as if the only reason I persisted was for fear of hurting others.

I have come to understand that transient moments of nearly breathtaking hope and possibility also come from this God. It was most surely this steadfast God who held and tended me when those trusted psychiatrists medicated me, sought to silence the little boy within me, dulled my memories, shamed my self-understanding, and submerged my selfhood in a fog of dissociation, stubborn survival, and compensatory over-functioning. So, too, it was this God—God of my Grandmother—who accompanied me, sustained me, and guided me when the people of *The Church* writ large and *their* God nearly killed me. It was Grandmother's God—*my God*—who kept me alive, accompanied me, and spoke to me in unconventional ways through the worst of my drinking and drugging, the three years it took me to make a year sober, as well as all the trials, challenges, and successes of sober living, trauma recovery, and generally living on. The God of my ancestors, of my Grandma Daught and so many others before her, is the God who abides and accompanies.

This God, it seems, is the milky-blue spirit-lubricant that enables and abides with all manner of holy skin-shedding. This God, who is many things and bears many names, is also the God of Thresholds and, thus, of threshold-crossing, boundary-dwelling peoples—for slipping-skin, too, is a kind of crossing over: an intentional movement from one place, one stage of becoming, one ill-fitting way of being, to another more fitting way of moving and being in the world.

Like crossing a stream—maybe, even the Jordan—entering the Sacred Grove is, itself, a passage. It is an act of passing through the surrounding landscapes that border and define its presence: crossing over the threshold of all that is "not the Grove" and moving into all that "is the Grove." To cross the threshold is to make passage through the forests, thickets, creeks, streams, or grassy fields that make the Grove-space a grove, share and contribute to its biodiversity, set it apart, and, simultaneously, connect it to the whole of life everywhere.

Like the earth to the cosmos, like human beings to the rest of the planet, the bordering lands and the grove itself are inseparable. One does not exist without the other. In a sense, groves and surrounding environments are not only mutually dependent; they are mutually creating. The spaces between them are thin and dynamic. Without the other, they each become something else. And so it is, in ways both mystical and mundane, moving between these spaces reveals that, ultimately, everywhere is threshold-crossing.

The constructed world and the natural world are threshold crossings. That is, like the thresholds of forests, fields, streams, and

groves, the natural world we have been given exists, interconnective-
ly, with the environments humans construct. These spaces, equally, describe and define each other—as well as the sometimes stark,
sometimes ever-so-thin, transitional spaces between them. Just as
grasses and plantlife resist concrete and asphalt, spouting up and
through these unnatural constructs in thriving displays of vitality,
our gender-transcendent lives resist the constructs designed to con-
cretize and constrict our most authentic manifestations of self-understanding.

Gender-transcendent persons are threshold-crossing beings
abiding in the spaces between the world of human constructs and the
world of Grove-remembering manifestation, where authentic personhood can take shape and, ultimately, comes of age. Were it not for
the constructed binaries that make us *other* and, ultimately, define us
as transgender, non-binary, intersex, or myriad other words for gender-expansive persons, we would no doubt be viewed by the world
as something else—perhaps as needful parts of the natural world.
We would slip out of the ill-fitting, unnatural skin of constructed
gender-*otherness* imposed upon us, and we would grow fully into the
distinctly diverse, particularly gendered, self-actualizing persons we
would naturally be and become.

However, for now, until such a time arrives, we remain threshold-crossing beings living at the borders of reductive constructs—
and, simultaneously, among the many oppressive marginalizations
built around and reinforcing those constructs. So too, we live at the
boundaries of our own vibrant, natural, gender-transcendent becoming and the world around us. What I mean to say is that we
grow and develop as persons, through naturally occurring stages,
transitions, and maturations while existing in, and navigating, a constructed world generally ill-equipped to nurture us. In compounding
ways, in becoming-consternating ways, we live at the boundaries of
the boundaries—the margins of the margins—as the identities and
social locations that make us *other* are many.

Gender-transcendent persons live at the confluence of iden-
tity-crushing power, the dislocations those layers of outsiderness

present, and the daily travails of moving through the world we inhabit. Our bodies bump against the power-maintaining scaffolds that frame the constructed order—such as race, class, gender, sex, ability, age, and a host of others. With every added layer, the weight and confined immobility increases, pushing our individual backs harder and harder against the walls around us. Each of our multiple identities positions us deeper and deeper into the press.

As such, we know something about being people of the margins; we know some things about recognizing the differences between naturally occurring boundaries and those arbitrarily created to exclude and oppress. Boundaries are the distinguishing features of beings, bodies, spaces, and things. They are important. We cannot just wish them away entirely.

We know, in our skin, something meaningful about marginalization and exclusion—and, by implication, we know about creating sanctuary Grove-spaces: places where we recollect a meaningful sense of self, where we center community, where we strive for relief, renewal, and flourishing. We recognize the transformative power in these ways of knowing and being. The wisdom-ways born in our experience carry not only life-changing, but world-changing potential—if only we might wrap our arms around that wisdom and make it plain. Yet, we know these things not because we strive for the power of the dominating culture, but in striving to respond to it through our endowed, personal power—because our survival demands responding in ways that are life-promoting, to the press of power enacted against us.

Engaging the process of moving such knowledge into the world is, itself, a process that entails slipping the skins imposed upon us, like pulling away years of undergrowth, fallen limbs, leaves, and brush to reveal a hidden path to a wide, burgeoning Grove-space, just beyond our line of sight. Becoming more and more intentional about employing our margin-detecting and maneuvering abilities prepares us to reveal renewed and shiny layers of who we are underneath the constructed mythologized-skins in which we are often trapped. Naming the realities of our lives and telling the wisdom carried in our individual and collective stories are processes through which we reveal ourselves. We share discovered insights that, in turn, make visible the many false skins ascribed to us, to our world, and to others who inhabit it with us. When we move such vital knowledge into the world around us, it is a process of shedding skin. We shed the narrative veils that cover, too, the world we inhabit (and which equally, through enculturation, *inhabit* us).

What I mean to say is this: like others who dwell in the borderlands between the world of colonizing, constructed mythologies and the fertile ground of our natural selves, we know how to learn from our surroundings. We read the signs and signals around us, and respond accordingly. We have to, because, too often, there are severe consequences for failing to recognize such signs. We know how to discern when to camouflage, when to blend in, as well as when to reveal our real selves, when to share our true skin. In other words, we know when to shed. We know how to do all of this because we have felt the biting sting of harsh and predatory reactions.

The truth is, shedding ill-fitting skin is something we instinctively know how to do. Like distinguishing predators from friends, slipping skin is a natural ability, and it is a necessary part of *becoming* our most authentic, individuated selves. Shedding skin is a truly miraculous, necessary, and recurring process. It is also a kind of gift, a facility—though not for the faint of heart. Sometimes even snakes have trouble doing it. Sometimes, even a snake will get stuck in its ill-fitting skin. There are so many lessons to be learned from the grove and all its surrounding, entryway thresholds. Shedding skin is a valuable lesson—one we know in our Grove-born skin.

chapter seven

Holy Set-Apartness

And the Existing One said to Abram:
"Go; go forth from your land, and from the place
of your birth, and from the house of your relatives,
to a land I will show you."
Genesis 12:1
author's translation

Therefore, you are to be holy ones to me,
for I, the Existing One, am holy;
and I have separated you from the peoples to be mine.
Leviticus 20:26
author's translation

Threshold crossing is, in a sense, fundamental to all transitional and transformative experiences—be it shedding skin or stepping from tangled forest thicket into the sheltered opening of a grove. This is a knowledge we hold in our very bodies. Perhaps, this metaphoric truth is why journeying, crossing over, being set apart, and making sanctuary spaces lie at the heart of the call, experience, and very being of the Hebrew people.

In fact, as the stories tell, beginning with Abraham, the overarching story of the Jewish people is a cyclical story of taking leave, sojourning, receiving revelations, renewing self-discovery, reflecting, and returning. Abram's story begins with the voice of God, saying "Go! Leave your home, all that you know, and go to a place I will

69

show you" (Genesis 12:1). Along the way in his journey with God, Abram receives a new name, Abraham, and God's promise that all the peoples of the world will be blessed through him. From Abraham onward, the stories of the Hebrew people become both spiritual journey and spiritual allegory.

Theirs are stories of being called by God to journey from birth-places to new places; to sojourn in some kind of wilderness; and to cross rivers, borders, and social conventions in answer to a call to be God's people. Most significantly, the leave-taking is always followed by a return to the world of others with a renewed self-understanding, revelations of the nature of covenant relationship with God and each other, and deepened commitment to discerning what it means to be God's people. In each wilderness sojourn, revelations are given and received; in returning to community, gifts and wisdoms to be found in practice and experience are revealed. Perhaps, we too are people called to cross all manner of rivers, borderland thresholds, and social conventions. I propose that we are like Abraham and the ancient Hebrew people in just this kind of way.

In Genesis 14:13, we find the first mention of the word *Ivri*, which we come to translate and understand as "Hebrew." Here, the story tells us that a refugee came to relate information about Lot to "Abram, the Hebrew." The root of this word *Ivri* (or "Hebrew") is *avar*, which means "to pass over, through, by, or pass on." The adjective form, *ivri*, means "one from beyond; from the other side." This is fitting, as Abram is believed to have come from the other side of the river, but it is also theologically significant as Abram became one who was literally "on the other side" of socioreligious convention in his choice to follow this One-God, his God, the One who would come to be called the God of Abraham. This choice not only begins the monotheistic faith of Judaism; it is also the beginning of the Hebrew people and their continually evolving, distinct journey with God.

Thus, the word *Ivri* itself becomes a one-word signifier of a people set apart. It is a living allegory for a continuing sojourn with God: for hearing a call to take leave from the conventional world; for crossing the threshold, to the other side, into a wilderness rich with trials, sustenance, discoveries, and lessons in becoming—and of learning to build community. *Ivri* is an allegory for receiving life-way revelations and for returning, passing over again, to be in the world but not of it, to be always, intentionally, "on the other side" and set apart. In this way we gender-transcendent peoples, too, are an *Ivri* of a sort: threshold-crossing, boundary-transgressing, set-apart people sojourning in a wilderness with our God.

The Hebrew people transgressed—and continue to transgress—contrived social and religious boundaries. In doing so, they developed unique ways of distinguishing and working with naturally occurring and created boundaries. This became the basis of a continuing way of life intent on seeking to understand, achieve, and maintain holiness. Toward these ends, they also became spiritual boundary-*setters*, developing particular ways of thinking about God and covenant relations, as well as rituals and religious practices that are visible, distinguishable signs of their set-apartness.

As gender-transcendent folk, we, too, hear a call to intentionally transgress conventions, discern a unique and particular life-way, and set for ourselves a range of boundaries necessary for personal growth, health, safety, and ongoing self-actualization. And, like the Hebrew people, we call attention to and invite consideration of ways in which our personal experiences and insights can be culled together in the creation of a meaningful sense of peoplehood—perhaps, even, a peoplehood in abiding relationship with a One-God. This God of the gender-transcendent *Ivri* must be vast enough, free enough from limiting doctrine and dogma, to hold all of us and all our many relational and experiential understandings of God—a God who teaches us, by relational example, how to make spaces wide enough to embrace each other. While we may, indeed, form small communities of kindred, we too are still learning how to be a people, bound not only by set-apartness, but also by innate, vibrant diversity. In many ways, even as we struggle to free ourselves, individually, from all manner of ill-fitting skins, we struggle, too, to slip the judgmental, exclusionary, divisive skins into which we have been stuffed, zipped-up, and enculturated.

Among the many vexing conditions outcast peoples face, it seems, is the unconscious, assimilated tendency to do with and to each other what has been done to us. Quite possibly, this is so in large part because it is so difficult to learn to refrain from reproducing, internally, upon our own selves, all the harmful messages and ways of being that have been conditioned into us. These realities call us to access all our ways of knowing so we might remember we are graceful, glorious Grove-born people, that we are more than enough as we are. Seeking to be our fullest selves teaches us to shed not only false-gender skins, but all the ill-fitting skins that prevent us from becoming, more fully, who we are.

The more we accept and affirm ourselves, the more we are able to accept one another. For we know, too well, that attempting to control and conscribe individual self-understanding and identity is, ultimately, the most arrogant of human attempts to subordinate and control not only others but nature itself (and especially God). By attempting to dictate who people are—who people are allowed to be in their own bodies, in their own self-understandings—human agents exceed the reaches of their power and make of themselves "gods." Such violations of natural boundaries are, in the end, the folly of human arrogance, for these dictations violate not only the bare and breathtaking, individuation of nature, but also violate the boundaries of holiness.

As the Genesis stories describe from the beginning, Holy Otherness created natural boundaries, *rather than margins*, within all of creation—the evening and the morning, the lands and the waters, the creatures of the air, and even the conspicuous boundaries between human beings. Boundaries signal and denote distinctive individuations and the relationality born within those natural states. God teaches us about sacred relationships by abiding in and working with those boundaries between Godself and us. God comes seeking us, calling us into relational connection—not into subjugation but into valued acceptance; not into controlling expectation but into hopeful anticipation of who we might choose to be; not into boxed-up, constrictive ways of being but into affirmed, endowed personhood.

To be clear, there is an important distinction among God's obvious affinity for diversity, God's preservation of individuated freedom, and God's understanding that human beings, and all created things as well, need natural boundaries. Natural boundaries distinguish one person from another, one thing from another, preserve relational individuality, and enable the growth and development necessitated by our becoming. In this world, mountains do not go moving about like bipedal beings, though they may make certain kinds of decisions that occur far beyond our limited understanding. Human beings do not sprout trees from our shoulders, though we can certainly put our arms to work planting trees. Differences are not theoretical. Boundaries are meaningful.

Said more pointedly, not every impulse we might have is healthy for us, for others, or for creation. Not every behavior is something we are preserved, honored, or cared for by committing it. There are important distinctions between behaviors and personhood. Still, our Creator allows and preserves our freedom to choose. We, as beings, are not the sum of our behaviors, yet the forms and types of behaviors we are able to commit derive from, and are boundaried by, our being human beings rather than something else. We, like everything else, need boundaries appropriate to our particular nature. Humans, therefore, need social agreements, some measure of mutually protective guidelines for conduct and engagement, and parameters for assuring that the flourishing of some does not exploit or impede the flourishing of others.

The whole of our sacred stories combine to express an understanding that God does not make endless automaton copies of identical sameness. God is not a puppet master. God created, and preserves, an ever-evolving diversity of things and beings. And, always, like grass pushing out through breaks in a concrete slab, the freedom of individuation and self-determination is preserved so that an individual can choose to cross over into authentic relationships. Individuation, relationality, and holiness are intimately bound.

The Hebrew concept of holiness is expressed by the word *kodesh*, which means "apartness" or "sacredness," and, thus, holiness or sanctity. The verb form, *kadash*, means "to be set apart, to be holy, sacred,

73

and/or consecrated." Likewise, the adjective, *kadosh*, describes a person, a being, or a thing that is sacred or holy. Thus, to be set apart is to be consecrated, to be made holy. Likewise, striving for holiness implies a willingness to be formed and transformed in ways that involve some measure of set-apartness, of distinction.

It could be said that to intuit a call to be set apart in a distinct relationship with God, and to choose to live in such a way, is a manifestation of the Levitical command to "be holy as God is holy" (Leviticus 20:26). Repeatedly, in Chapters 19–21 of Leviticus, God instructs the people to "be holy" because *God is holy* and reminds them they have been set apart, as a people, to be in a particular relationship with a set-apart, Wholly-Other God. That is, they are chosen to be in a specific, differentiated relationship with Holiness—not God's *only* people, but a particular people of God. Perhaps, the same is true for us. It strikes me that these images hold powerful implications regarding what it means to be made in God's likeness and image.

Admittedly, the idea that we, as humans, are images of God is a point of personal reflection and meaning-making. Indeed, it consumes most of my theological musings and investigations. Still, it seems to me that we, as gender-transcendent people, are more near to God, in likeness and being, than we might imagine. The more "other" we are, the more transcendently true this may be. God is, after all, the Original Other; God is the first one set apart and holy.

God is the Knowable *and* Unknown Stranger within and among us. God is oddly near to us, as close as our own God-inspired breath, yet God is wholly beyond us. This One God is peculiar to us, strange and nearly incomprehensible, and yet, sometimes, mysteriously familiar and accessible to us. God is a felt presence in our experiences, yet God is not here, in this room, in this place, or anywhere we can tangibly discern. Still, we are infused with longing for Jacob moments of our own—dawning recognitions that the Existing One was here, in this place, all along, and we did not even know. God is decidedly odd. God who is presumably transcendent and unafflicted by human dispositions and needs, still seems to need us in nearly incomprehensible ways. This God who could, no doubt, ignore us altogether, or even do away with us, appears to be invested in our survival. God is queer, in-deed. This One is not like anything else we know or understand, not like anything familiar. And yet, Holy Otherness makes some measure of God's peculiar self familiar to humans across time, culture, and history. This queer stranger, this God who is foreign to us, is also the Sustaining Spirit who is always with us, abiding among and around us, seeking us, and drawing us out of our hiding places. God is ever in-dwelling and yet not us, always near us and also far beyond us.

God is the original Boundary-Crossing *Oneness*, who transcends the limitations of human theological assumptions; passing through hearts, minds, and communities, but mysteriously leaving behind something of Godself everywhere. Perhaps this residual otherness is like a remnant of God-skin, the skin that God has shed for us. God, it seems, is the Skin-slipping Whisperer of Revelations, always shedding ill-fitting attributes and definitions; existing and disclosing Godself from beyond the many familiar conventions, doctrines, dog-mas, and religious traditions. In these ways, we share something of God's likeness as *Other*. We, too, transcend imposed limitations placed upon us. We push against assumptions made about us and transcend confines, slipping through cracks in the concrete. Like God, we cross human assumptions, pass through hearts, minds, and communities, and miraculously leave behind something of ourselves in the process. The more strangely peculiar, oddly individuated, queerly distinct, and *other* we are, the more we are like the Holy Other in whose image we are created. If we recognize ourselves in these images and accept their truthfulness, we just might accept that our skin-slipping gifts can bring us nearer to our God—not only in our *otherhood*-likeness to God, but also in our relationship with this Holy Otherness. And, perhaps, nearer to each other.

If so, then we can rightly claim our intentional sojourns toward authentic selfhood are sacred sojourns, holy journeys. Our intention-al participation in our own trans-formational becoming not only sets us apart not only because of how others view and treat us, but also because we have consented to hear and heed the God who calls us into being. Like our ancestors in that first set-apart Sacred Garden, we hear the rustling of the Holy Other passing by, on some breezy evening, calling us to become more ourselves. We hear God asking, "Where are you?" (Genesis 3:9) and we understand our Creator is calling us into conspicuous personhood—calling us to show ourselves, to come out of hiding, to live boldly into our set-apartness, our distinctiveness, and to manifest a flourishing sense of selfhood in connection-seeking relationship to all that is.

Perhaps, we are more like God than we've dared imagine. As well, we are more like the holy set-apart otherness of the germinal Grove in which we come into being than we know. This God, the Creator of the Sacred Grove, comes seeking us and claims each one of us as God's own set-apart people. From the *other side*, God calls to us—the threshold-crossing, skin-slipping, margin-dwelling people of the Sacred Grove, made to be and placed, *on the other side* of the world of human constructs. We, the Grove of being, and God, too, are all *ivri*. And so it is, our gender-transcendent set-apartness is a particular state of holiness.

I offer these reflections to say, and affirm, this: there are many ways to shed skin, to make crossings, and, like crossing from world to Grove and back again, these transitional processes are connected. Each crossing is needful for becoming who we are; each made necessary by ill-fitting constructs and prescribed ways of being that are unbefitting a natural world of endless becoming, interconnectivity, and relationality. This need to shed all that is not us to become our most authentic selves is a gift, a facility, and an aptitude—magical and magnificent. It is an undertaking in sacred set-apartness. Each movement we make toward fully actualized, authentic selfhood is a shedding of old, restrictive skin. Each step we make toward our own becoming is a crossing over, a passage through the thin space between the stories imposed upon us about who we can be—who we are permitted to be—and who we, in fact, know ourselves to be.

Every effort we make toward creating sanctuary spaces of solidarity, support, and mutual thriving is an active, intentional loosing of the skins that cover us in a world that, at best, seeks to thwart our becoming and, at worst, seeks to erase us. Each time we move in freedom from the world of false, binding constructs, we cross over into the Sacred Grove of a natural, authentic state of being. There, amid the comfort of sacred trees, grasses, and rocks, we slip the skin of *ascribed otherness*, and rest in warm, sun-drenched connection with our set-apart kindred—if only for the moment. Crossing over from one place to another comes naturally to us, for we are boundary-dwelling threshold-crossers, who transgress forces of confinement. Slipping skin is second-nature to us because we, like our serpent kindred, are wise bearers of skin-shedding, trans-formative magic.

There are so many ways to make crossings. So, too, there are many ways to shed skin. Indeed, there are many forms of skin-shedding beings. It is interesting to note, the verb form of the Hebrew word for serpent is *nachash* and means: "to practice divination" (with the implied power to learn secret things); "to divine, or observe signs"; or "to make enchantments"; and especially, "to hiss, to whisper, and particularly, to whisper divinations." Doubtless, there are also many ways to divine secret things and to whisper wise proclamations.

As gender-transcendent persons, we know a little something about these themes—not only about journey-making and shedding skin, but also about discerning secrets and whispering wisdom. And, these things—these wisdoms gained through experience; these gleanings from miraculous, skin-slipping trans-formations, shared, whispered, and lived; these knowledge-ways—are also holiness ways. They are ways of being set apart and of growing closer to the Holy Other. They have life-changing and world-transforming power.

These are our gifts, waiting to be embraced in full. These are our gifts to the world we inhabit. These are our gifts to one another. Our skin-slipping facilities and wisdoms emerge in the narrows of oppression, but this also is true of many other beautiful, transformative, world changing things. We are free to use these gifts. We are *invited*, perhaps *called*, to use these gifts, to divine and to discern how we—each of us, individually, and gatherings of us, collectively—choose to manifest our gifts as we cross thresholds, bringing our Trans-Forming Proclamations into the world.

chapter eight

Beyond the Gates of the City

The word of the Lord came to Elijah [him]: "Go from here,
and turn eastward, and hide yourself by the Wadi Cherith, which is
east of the Jordan. You will drink from the wadi, and I
have commanded the ravens to sustain you there."
And he went and he did according to the word of God: he went, and he
dwelled by the Wadi Cherith which is east of the Jordan.

The ravens brought him bread and meat every morning
and bread and meat every evening, and from the wadi, he drank.
And it was after some time, the day came the wadi dried up
because there was no rain in the land. And it was, the
word of God spoke to him, "Rise up; go at once to
Zarephath which is toward Sidon, and dwell there.
Behold, I have designated a widow there to sustain you."

1 Kings 17:2–9
author's translation

Outside the gates of the city proper, scatterings of entire worlds exist beyond the sight and awareness of average day-to-day persons living, working, and going about their lives. These worlds interact, gravitationally in a sense; they communicate, sometimes touch, collide, and merge together, as do all the world-forming atoms, molecules, elements, and compounds present and imaginable. Worlds upon worlds exist, beyond the gates, and these matter because worlds *are* matter. These outlying worlds manifest all the wholeness of life—

combining, merging, and bearing-forth all the fullness of stardust elemental matter into particular, distinct living bodies—just as any other world. Like galaxies within the vastness of the universe, these living worlds are cast beyond the fixed orbs of cities, townships, and gated communities in our earthly world and, therefore, lie beyond the awareness and concern of other life-budding, surrounding worlds.

These worlds, existing beyond the gates of the city proper, are human beings set to the margins crafted in the mundane world of intentionally constructed borderlands. As well, there are far-flung composite earthbound universes, like star clusters, consisting of gathered groups of cast-out peoples—living their daily lives, striving, surviving, and making transit, always crossing over the thresholds between personal home-spaces, grove spaces, and city gates of all kinds, in all places. We, too, in our diverse ways, are outlying human worlds beyond the gates of the glowing orb of the valued city. And we, too, matter because we *are* matter—particular, individuated, diversely unique manifestations of eternal stardust, living and moving in an earthly universe of ill-fitting, imposed mythologies. Yet, we are not alone. There are always other outcast strangers near to us, for we are those made other in many interconnected ways.

Outside the city gates, we are scattered within the many peoples also made strangers by the same forces of colonization and white supremacy that lord presumed superiority over so many, using gender, race, class, religion, and a whole host of unholy empire-supporting ways of othering. Just beyond the gates, there are communities of Black and Brown persons cast out from meaningful shares in the rights, resources, and protections provided to the privileged. We, too, are there—gender-transcendent persons living on at the borderland margins. Cast out, everywhere, beyond the many gates built on stolen land, communities of Indigenous persons live and strive for sovereign bodiedness, lands, personhood, and nation-status. There, too, are we—diverse, gender-transcendent, Indigenous persons living on. Beyond the gates, there are collectives of immigrant persons, gathered from many lands, cultures, and heritages. And we are there too—particular, miniature worlds among worlds. And, we are among them all.

In the clusters of outcast communities beyond the city proper, there are communities of impoverished persons, disabled persons; forgotten elders, young people, and everyone in between, living in food deserts, in high-rises, in housing insecurity, and even in tents and on park benches. There, too, we are gathered among the outcasts. Each and every one of us, equally, is a living, bodied, and vibrant human world.

Beyond the gates of the cities are other forgotten persons among forgotten peoples. There are those who suffer addictions and chronic illnesses, and others who struggle to achieve and maintain mental, emotional, and spiritual wellness. There are those who are without a permanent home. Beyond the proper cities are a host of diverse, individual persons who are wonderful weirdos, fabulous freaks, glorious geeks, and folks with interesting eccentricities who, too, have been deemed outcast strangers. There are persons who are sex workers; those who are librarians (yes, there are still librarians), restaurant workers and, even, store-front psychics. There are carnies, street musicians, wandering poets, various artists, and a whole host of other travelers. And we gender-transcendent persons are most surely among these peoples as well. For we are, indeed, an ancient people who come from many lands, many cultures, heritages, and traditions, gifted and equipped with various skills, talents, knowledge-ways, and wisdoms. And each of us, like all the persons around us—each and every marvelously gender-transcendent one of us—is a living world, entirely.

We are often forgotten by the power-holders and the makers of public stories, yet we are not necessarily forgotten one to another. We, the forgotten, have not forgotten. We are all too aware that outside the gates of the city, entire worlds are devalued, neglected, mistreated, tossed away into desolation, and, all too often, destroyed. There is freedom but also danger outside the gates of the city. We, as gender-transcendent persons are endangered—not only because we are gender-transcendent, but because our other identities make us vulnerable. Collectively and individually, we are increasingly aware of the layered identity-based terrors, afflictions, and perils facing us. We live in a society built upon the destructive connections between the commodification, appropriation, and exploitation of land and natural resources, and the commodification, appropriation, and exploitation of human bodies. We are colonized, endangered people striving to live on colonized and endangered lands.

These realities call us to reimagine how we think about and relate to the land that sustains us—this earth that sustains the eternal Grove and all the other groves, forests, gardens, waters, and life born from it. More pointedly, these realities call us to recenter and reimagine a vision of each embodied person as a world, entire and complete—to consider the truth of the body as a living, creation-consisting world, as *place*, as selfhood-endowed homeland, and therefore deserving of care, nurture, and cultivation, and most especially, necessitating and demanding a measure of sovereignty. Bodies, like land, cannot thrive without being tended, cultivated, and nurtured.

Though I am certainly proposing a certain expansive proclamation here—the proclamation of our individual bodies as places, as sacred, sovereign homelands—the idea of each human being manifesting as an entire, living world is ancient wisdom. The Jewish sages say that every person is *olam katan*—a miniature world (*Midrash Tanchuma, Pekudei - Siman 3*). Moreover, each person—each *olam katan*—is also *olam malei*, a *complete*, entire world. That is, each person is a living, selfhood-endowed microcosm of all the divinity-infused elemental contents of the entire cosmos. We are, at once, in the universe and the whole universe is in us. We are the stuff of creation. And, most surely, as unique gender-transcendent persons, we especially are testaments to the vast, unfettered natural diversity of everything that is. We are in the Grove, and the Grove is in us.

Everything in the cosmos, every *thing* that is, is connected to everything else. Made of the same sacred stuff of creation, everything consists of and exists in the cosmic everywhere-nowhere. And so, every single life matters. Every single living thing, and especially every human being, matters because all that lives *is* the matter of creation. Thus, the Talmudic sages teach us that anyone who sustains one individual has acted to sustain an entire world; anyone who destroys an individual person has acted to destroy the world (Sanhedrin 37a). Each and every human life has value and significance as a miniature world unto a larger, wider, shared world consisting of interdependent distinctiveness and diversity.

Every human being is a temple made of blood and spirit, skin and bone, and breath. Every single person, then, is endowed with gifts, wisdom, understanding, and knowledge. More, these qualities originate in the indwelling God. Further, as complete personhood-endowed houses of Holiness, then the understandings, knowledge-ways, and wisdoms of every single human, tabernacle-being are holy and sacred as well. Thus, the wisdom, understanding, and knowledge of every human being matter—to the whole of creation and to God—because these, too, *are* matter: the matter, it seems, of the whole of creation *and* of God. Further, then, it could be said that anyone who destroys a single human being destroys, also, not only individuated human-world particles of creation, but also destroys some measure of the *particles of God.* Whoever sustains a single human being has acted to sustain, not only some embodied portion of the elements of creation, but also a *human measure of the differentiated particles of God.*

How much more true is this of unseen, unrecognized, and even despised gender-transcendent outcast persons whose very presence in the world at large recalls the primal Sacred Grove—and in so doing, recalls the God of the Garden-Grove? How much more is this true for gender-transcendent persons who are mistreated, violated, and murdered? How much more is this true for us, as gender-transcendent persons, whose experiences, knowledge-ways, and wisdoms are necessary, yet largely unrecognized, contributions to the formation of a deeper, more nuanced understanding of all that inheres in being a human being?

The value of a single human life, particularly those cast out beyond the gates of the city, speaks through the story of Elijah, the widow woman, and her son. In this short tale, God acts to provide for these single, individual persons the same kinds of care, protection, and sustaining interventions God enacted for the entire Hebrew people, including the outcast strangers they took with them in the flight from Egypt. This God, it seems, favors and advocates for those made outcast strangers over those who make of themselves kings. God collaborated, equally and intentionally, with nature, created beings, and human agents for the sole purposes of saving *one* single prophet, *one* widow, and *one* little boy.

Specifically, God worked providentially through the natural world to sustain Elijah, then worked through the elements of flour and oil to save not only Elijah but the widow and her son as well. God made use of the seasonal wadi, or stream, to assure Elijah had water to drink. Miraculously, at the same time, God instructed the ravens there to bring meat and bread to Elijah in the morning and again in the evening. If Elijah was, in any way, unsettled by the idea of being fed by ravens as he hid by the wadi, that apprehension is absent in the story. For Elijah, such strange providence did not seem at all unusual.

In many ways, this is not surprising. People who live beyond the margins of the city gates are not only accustomed to, but are adept at, receiving sustenance and support through creative, unconventional means and, often, through delivery by unexpected sources—perhaps even, sources those people privileged with position and resources deem to be strange, unusual, outright unsavory, sordid, or disreputable.

Said another way, life at the margins creates and informs strikingly different views of reality and experiences of survival, sustenance, alliances, support, and potential thriving than does life in the lofty palace of a king. It is also true that, in the worldview of these biblical stories, God is at the center of a vibrant, somewhat magical, unity of interrelated things, beings, and forces above the palaces of kings. It is significant to the project of dreaming and intentionally crafting a Trans-Forming Proclamation that the beings who tend to Elijah are ravens—birds not valued by elite, respectable standards, but, nonetheless, one of the oldest, most adaptive, resilient, and creative species of birds. And, like gender-transcendent people (and other marginalized folk), they are often feared.

Ravens—like us, in a primary way—are, in fact, found all over the world and adapt to living in the most extreme and inhospitable environments and conditions. A glance at any online encyclopedia reveals that there are about ten species of these large, heavy-billed, dark birds belonging to the genus *Corvus*. Although ravens are typically thought to be purely black in color, their feathers actually bear iridescent, dark blue and purple hues. When viewed closely, the colors are striking, beautiful. There are even white-necked western North American ravens. Generally, ravens are also quite intelligent and have a large, varied bird vocabulary. In rather impressive displays of intelligence, they have been observed to utilize found items as tools, demonstrating capacity for forethought, complex and purposeful reasoning, and planning for the future. Common raven species are even known to retrieve items they deem valuable and save them for barter and trade later, when advantageous. Ravens display rather stunning flight maneuvers and soaring aerial acrobatics during courtship. Though generally solitary, ravens often feed in small flocks. It could be said, although they are introverts, ravens work together and help one another.

Generally diminished as scavengers, in truth, ravens are omnivores and only feed on carrion, carcasses, and discarded foods when they have to in order to survive. Especially worth noting, here, ravens have historically held a special status among many peoples of the old religions and among various Indigenous peoples; they are generally revered as heraldic prophets of a sort, portending death, diseases, or other natural catastrophes. Ravens, too, like people of a certain call and vocation, warn of things to come. Mystically speaking, ravens have been understood to be transdimensional beings. For this, like us, as surely as they have been revered, ravens have been feared. Thus, like us, they are Grove creatures, existing well beyond the city gates, yet always, crossing over thresholds, seen and unseen.

It could be said, perhaps, that they are transdimensional, transformation-portending prophet familiars.

The presence of ravens as the bearers of care and sustenance not only demonstrates that Creator-God deems all life as sacred; it also emphasizes the many ways that every living being bears particular talents, gifts, and value—at any time, in spectacular, unique, and often surprising ways, God engages and collaborates with even the most unlikely accomplices in the work of dreaming into being a world to come. At the very least, the God portrayed in this story demonstrates a set of values and priorities above those held within the courts of kings.

To this God, creation matters because the whole of creation *is* matter—in fact, God-particle matter. For God, no element of creation—be it seasonal wadi, grain for bread, or plot of ground to grow it—is expendable. No member of creation is too small, too weak, too unlikely, or too strange to participate in the good of God's cosmic household. Moreover, *no single person is expendable.* Elijah's tale draws on intentionally chosen and carefully placed characters to call unmistakable attention not only to God's life-sustaining cooperation and collaboration with the stuff and beings in the natural world, but equally, to the ways oppressed, abused, and forgotten people are marginalized into spaces that necessitate learning to recognize, collaborate with, and come to care for one another. The overarching proclamation lived in Zarephath is twofold: that no single person is too small, too unlikely, too strange, or too undeserving to be of value and contribution to God's dreams of an Eden-invoking world; and such Eden-dreaming, relational cooperation with God, nature, and one another constitutes the way that God desires for us to live.

Thus, as notable as it is that God collaborated with ravens to sustain a prophet in hiding, it is equally notable that, when the wadi ran dry, God placed Elijah in the care of a destitute widow, impoverished of resources and of hope. God chose a stranger—a resident outsider, slowly wasting away outside the gates of the city. As is often the case among outcast peoples beyond the city proper, Elijah and the woman were thrust together in a cooperative mutuality of need. Each of them was placed in a position of either trusting the other and working together—or going it alone and perishing alone. Elijah was called to trust the widow would consent and help him, and she was called to trust that Elijah would not harm her or her son. Moreover, together, they were called into a communal faith that God would, indeed, assure there would be enough resources for them all to survive.

And, so it was; there was enough. The nearly-empty bowl of flour and jar of oil became a bounty. These, it seems, are the miracles born through relational collaborations—between God and natural materials, between God and circumstances, between God and individual people, and, most surely, between particular people who find themselves together in unlikely interdependent relationships.

Doubtless, for these three, bread would have been enough, yet outside the city proper, God's providence expands, spreads, rises up like sourdough. For Elijah and the widow and her son, a synergy of mutual need and cooperation saved them all. And, the widow's trust of Elijah, in defiance of all apparent reason, assured that Elijah was there to heal the widow's son when, later, he took ill. This is an essential point in the story. Unless we are willing to be in relationship with one another, and, especially, unless we are willing to work together to sustain one another, we may inadvertently harm ourselves—perhaps, even, our children. Quite possibly, the way we work, together, or apart, will either harm or save our children's children, literally and metaphorically. In God's cosmic social order, it seems, the sanctity of life and principles of interdependence reign above the seats of kings, and *every particular, individual person* is worth feeding, sheltering, sustaining, and saving—no matter who they are, what their circumstances, or where they come from. Still, we borderland-dwelling peoples, living on beyond the city gates, know how slow the collected peoples in human societies are to learn these truths.

The stark reality we know in our daily lives persists: that social policies and practices built upon the false premises of exceptionalism and privileging are, in fact, widow-makers, orphan-makers, and makers of all manner of outcasts, strangers, and impoverished peoples in need of relief from exclusion and abuse. Binary systems of all kinds are makers of outcast strangers. As such, these realities are also prophet-makers. And, prophets remind us that oppressive social systems violate the foundational assumptions of creation: that creation and everything within it—every element, every creature, every God-particle, molecule-manifesting thing, and, especially, *every human being—is an indispensable image of God.* Even, and especially, the seemingly strange, odd, wonderfully unusual humans among us.

Understanding these teachings through our gender-transcendent lives affirms that our living on does, indeed, proclaim beautiful and world-transforming propositions. Most especially, that every individuated human being is *olam katan*—that diversity of being is the foundation of the divine cosmic order, and therefore essential to the preservation and flourishing of all life. We proclaim that both the complexities of differences *and* of likenesses inform a deep understanding of human nature; and that gender-transcendent lives, in particular, are equally sacred, indispensable living parts of a wildly and marvelously diverse, interconnected, creation-affirming humanity, reflective of a diversity-drenched, interdependent cosmic reality. Our lives testify that we, too, contribute unique, wise, and necessary experiences, stories, knowledge-ways, and wisdoms to the continually evolving human search for God, for one another in vibrant communal connection, and, especially, for justice.

Elijah and the widow of Zarephath were not only strangers in the world of kings, they were also strangers to each other. They had, in fact, little in common, though personal experiences of desperation set them on a small patch of common ground, together, beyond the gates of the city proper. At any time, either of them could have gone their separate ways. The widow could have turned away—refusing to hear the voice calling to her, failing to see the human tabernacle before her who was, like her and her son, in need of sustenance. Elijah could have kept on moving. Mutual need bound them together in relational connection that gave rise to mutual benefit. Because of Elijah, the widow and her son survived. And, because a widowed mother consented to giving him shelter, Elijah discovered that not only his own survival but also the survival of the liberative message he was called to proclaim, were bound up in her living on.

In an ongoing living proclamation, Elijah, the widow, and her son join in contemporary concert with Black trans women, men, and non-binary persons; undocumented gender-transcendent persons; other trans and non-binary people of color; Two Spirit and other Indigenous persons beyond male and female; disabled gender-transcendent persons; and a wholly-holy host of other variously disenfranchised trans youth, elders, women, and queer persons who are cast out to the margins beyond the gates of the cities. Collectively, these voices call out to us—demanding that we work together to dismantle the very conditions that cast all of us as *olam katan*, bodied tabernacles to the borderland margins of the cities, townships, and neighborhoods around us. Their collective outcry calls us to reimagine what constitutes the means of a dignified, humanity-affirming life of flourishing for every person born in the land. Their voices call us to reflect, practically, and to reimagine the collective power to be found in recognizing and proclaiming the realities of embodied selfhood—of the body as sovereign place, as fleshy-homeland landscape, and therefore, as a holy tabernacle of skin and bone, blood and spirit. These collective voices—spoken in this sacred story and in the lives among us—call us to search for, discover, and work to bring into the ill-fitting, tabernacle-disregarding world an ever-widening sanctuary Grove that demonstrates inspired, revolutionary ways for creating more sustaining groves in the world we inhabit.

Ultimately, the story of Elijah and the widow implies what we—and all prophets worth their mantles—know: that if we were to create a world where every bodied person is valued as a complete, living, and vibrant holy temple, there would be no starving widows and children, no resident aliens, no strangers, no outcast persons deemed least-of-these, no left-behind and forgotten wanderers, and no need for prophets seeking sanctuary.

In the same tradition of *olam katan*, Judaism conceives of such work as *tikkun olam*—repairing the world. Ultimately, repair of the earthly world begins, always, with the repair of each individual miniature world. It begins with the world of self, moves to the individual human worlds we encounter, and then extends into the vast, shared world we inhabit. This work begins, it seems, by learning to turn our gaze beyond the field of our own positions, to turn a listening ear, and to lean into regarding, considering, and learning from the strangers traveling among us outside the gates of the city.

For us especially, as persons cast far from the city proper, all our knowledge-ways and capacities for recognizing and caring for one another can be trans-formed into practical, world-changing ways of caring for others. Our wisdom-ways and abilities for sheltering one another are powerful insights that can be trans-formed for sheltering a host of cast-out strangers. Our ability to recognize one another can be trans-formed into ways of recognizing and regarding equally vulnerable others. Our abilities to feed, tend to and clothe, nourish and support one another are vital knowledge-ways that can be offered, reshaped, and reformed in the work of trans-forming our world. We are living, vibrant, wise, and knowledgeable miniature worlds uniquely prepared to participate in repairing the world around us. In the work of repairing the world, we are valuable participants because we understand that the world is made of particular, individuated worlds—and worlds matter because worlds are the matter of God.

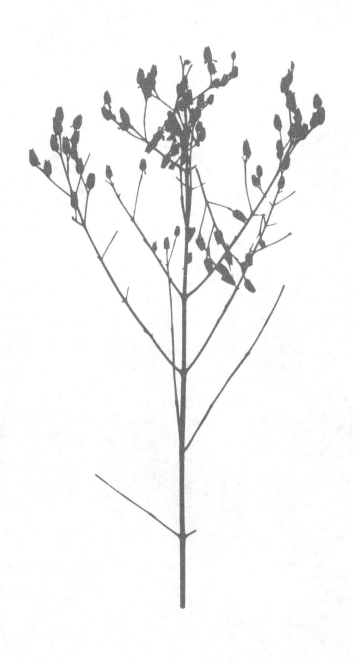

chapter nine

Taking Our Place
in the Divine Imaginary

Please ask the beast, however, and it will teach you,
and the bird of the heavens and it will tell you.
Or speak to the earth and it will teach you, and
the fish of the sea will declare to you.
Who among all of these does not know
that the hand of God made this,
in whose hand is the soul of every living thing
and the spirit-breath of all embodied persons?
Job 12:7–10
author's translation

How many are your works, Existing One,
in wisdom you made them all;
the earth is filled with your substance.
Psalm 104:24
author's translation

And God created the earth-being in God's own image,
in an image of God, God created … [the earthlings]
Genesis 1:27
author's translation

Throughout most of my formative years, my maternal grandparents lived in Arizona. My parents would scrimp and save all year so that, every summer when school was out, we could visit Grandma Daught and Grandpa. Although the messy nebula of my murky memory blends and blurs those individual visits into one sprawling cloud of images, those trips were some of the happiest times of my life. Not only were those visits love-filled, family vacations smattered with day trips and interesting things to do, but the time with my grandparents was also rich with opportunities for learning. Much of my learning has remained with me, shaping how I see the world, myself, and others, even if I cannot determine at which time, on what trip, I received the learning. It was on our trips to Arizona, through Grandma Daught's wise instruction and gentle guidance, that I internalized and began to understand that something of God comes to us everywhere, that all the earth is filled with the substance of God—and more, that every earthly thing, every earth-bound being, speaks valuable teachings.

From the time I was very young, I was fascinated with the natural world around me. When I was still toddling around, and even afterward, our trips to the free beaches near us were opportunities for curious, playful investigations of ocean creatures, shells, and sea-polished stones. On those days, I would sit in the water where the waves broke, facing the shore. As each rising wave washed over me, I would search all the salty treasures revealed by the ebbing water. Between the waves, I would gather up the tiny shells and stones I deemed worth saving and pile them up just beyond the reach of the coming waves. Then, I would settle back into the water and wait for the next cooling revelation of precious things. Hours would pass. Contentedly, I would search for artifacts of things beyond me—little things with large meaning. Equally at home in water and on land, I was also a tree-climber. Not only was there so much to see from the heights of a tree, but there were treasures to be found there too—pieces of hatched bird eggs, feathers, left-behind remains of nests, mosses, too, and loose leaves that never made it to the ground.

In Arizona, each summer, this natural disposition to love the earth and its riches expanded like sapling branches. Through guidance and teaching from my grandmother, especially, and my grandpa, I discovered a growing reverence for the way the ground, like our bodies, holds histories and for the seemingly endless offerings of wisdom in all that surrounds us. This engaged, curious reverence abides with me still—as does this lingering, growing belief there are teachings to be discerned in languages of earth, sky, water, plants, trees, and other creatures and beings. On some level, I think I've always known Job's author is correct. If we speak to the earth, it will teach us—not only, or merely, about the natural world, but about life and ourselves, as well. If there is one single lesson I learned from my grandmother, it would be to speak with and listen to the earth and all its elements, as well as the beasts, fishes, and birds.

Grandma kept bird feeders throughout the yard. I never tired of watching them, and Grandma never seemed to tire of teaching me. Mounted on a post on the back porch stairs, she kept a hummingbird feeder. Watching the quick, colorful, small-winged creatures mesmerized me. Hummingbirds taught me that, sometimes, a thing—even a life—can move so quickly, vibrating so intensely, it can appear to become completely still. Perhaps, even, to hover observantly over everything else. Often, my own life has been that way.

Similarly, from rabbits, I learned that, sometimes, stillness is protective. Life-saving. Sometimes, too, an intentional intensity of stillness is soul-protecting and nurturing. Hummingbirds and rabbits taught me about the strange relativity of time and its persistent fluidity. From fossils, I learned to notice the ways that time—that is, the history of time—resides in the body of the earth, all its many elements and all its living things: trees; mud, silt, sediment, and rocks; deserts, forests, streams, and even ancestral memory. The history of the world, the life of its time, lives on, and is held, in the aging, ever-renewing ground and all that springs forth from it. We, too, in our bodies, hold our own fossil record, our own history. Sometimes, we need to hover over the earth of our bodies, sense the home-place landscapes, and listen, intentionally, to hear the language our life is speaking. Other times, to discern the speech of our lives, we need to dig a little beneath the surface where the artifacts are found.

This is true about many things. This knowledge-way, I believe, is also a uniquely gender-transcendent way of knowing, interpreting, and discerning truth-bearing things. We know the wisdom of hummingbirds, like we know what the snake knows. We know the wisdom of rabbits. And, we know some things about searching the strange fleshy-fossil record of becoming, of bodied selfhood-landscapes, and of the many ways the evolving history of our personal, miniature world intersects and collides with other embodied, unfolding histories. Whether or not we might frame this knowledge in these ways, I suspect we also know that those who hate us, who fear and vilify us, have lost the ability to speak to the earth, to learn from it and from all our relations. Ungrounded in the origins of things, they also cannot learn from us.

The fearful makers of codified absolutes have forgotten that the Existing One formed everything in wisdom, that the whole earth and all it bears are filled with wise Holy Substance. They seem unaware, for example, that there are ten thousand species of true grasses, over which hummingbirds and ravens might fly, in which rabbits may nest, and skin-shedding snakes might take shelter.[2] Moreover, grasses—like the world, entire—continue to evolve. There is a growing number of named species of grasses awaiting full acceptance into the human-made classifications of grasses. Unmoved by this constructed limitation, grasses continue to proliferate and, quite often, sprout up amid and thrive alongside various other species of grasses.

At any given time, grasses are populated by one or more representatives of eleven thousand known species of grasshoppers, within the order *orthoptera*, and the suborder, *caelifera*—all of them, hopping, feeding, living, reproducing, and evolving within the many fields, groves, and meadows of diverse grasses and other foliages. I, personally, have seen at least two kinds of grasshoppers bounding

---

[2] To confirm the facts of my research into grasses, trees, and creatures in the natural world, I used the following sources: smithsonianmag.org; britannica.com; and nationalgeographic. com. All accessed between January 2020 and May 22, 2020. For more on trees, I recommend: Peter Wohlleben. *The Hidden Life of Trees: What They Feel, How They Communicate—Discoveries from a Secret World (The Mysteries of Nature)*. Greystone Books, 2016.

and hopping between brushy outcrops while hiking the Red Rocks in Arizona. I have watched, amusedly, as they hopped and flew from brush to tall grasses, to bushes and shrubs, and back again, amid a host of other, sometimes less interesting and sometimes more dangerous, insects.

Above the grasses throughout the world, in addition to ravens and, possibly, hummingbirds, one can expect to witness various representatives of more than ten thousand known species of birds, all flying, nesting, feeding, and reproducing among the many grasses, waterways, fields, and trees in our world. Since moving to my current home, some seventeen years ago, I have been gifted with the constant company of Carolina chickadees, sparrows, cardinals, wrens, robins, finches, crows, ravens, doves, and a brown-shouldered hawk who frequents the pecan tree, pines, and wood piles in my backyard. Occasionally, hummingbirds grace us with their presence. I have encouraged the company of our winged relations with feeders, particular plants and bushes, and attentive care of our trees.

Some years ago, I planted a butterfly bush near the screened porch. One day, at the start of the summer, I noticed a swarm of activity around the purple blooms. So, I moved closer, quietly, and stared with amazement at these tiny, beautiful, winged creatures hovering over the blossoms for nectar. At first glance, these brightly colored, shimmery souls looked like the smallest of young hummingbirds—that is, until I noticed they possessed antennae. These bird-like beings, I discovered, are hummingbird moths, also known as hawk-moths. These winged spirits were given their name because they have adapted and evolved to mimic the characteristics and abilities of their avian namesakes. Survival, it seems, breeds particular forms of intelligences. Like snakes and ravens, it seems, hummingbird moths too are our magical kindred familiars, carrying all manner of mystical trans-formative lessons and wisdom in their tiny, sheer-winged bodies. Unlike their cousins, however, hummingbird moths do not seem to nest in or frequent the branches of trees.

Nonetheless, there are over sixty thousand species of trees providing homes, food, and shelter to all types of birds, insects, and fur-bearing creatures—all of whom coexist, somewhat miraculously, together with all manner of grasshoppers, snakes, and other animals; bushes, shrubs, grasses, streams, and rivers. As a child, in Arizona, I was delighted to learn that saguaro cacti, despite their stunning appearance, are not in fact simply some prickly kind of trees. I was even more delighted to learn that some pears are actually prickly and when carefully harvested, as Grandma taught me, make a very fine jelly. However abundant in the west, prickly pears are also cacti, and therefore, like saguaros, are not trees. Once, after seeing pictures in a book, I asked Grandma if we could go see the trees that grow tall and fat in the desert and have all their branches on their tops. I was disappointed to learn that there were no baobab trees in the deserts of Arizona.

A few years ago, still taken with these curious trees, I read about baobabs and discovered they are often called the "tree of life" because they can store almost two thousand gallons of water, bear edible leaves, and produce nutrient-rich fruit. Thus, their intelligent adaptations prepare them to survive all sorts of travails, changes in climate, and droughts, assuring they provide water and food for humans and other life. Humans, if need be, can even take shelter in the center of the trees. A baobab tree can live up to three thousand years. Given this, it is likely that the oldest living baobab tree has outlived the push of empires, and is certainly older than the empire of Christendom. No doubt, some of our gender-transcendent ancestors walked among the baobab groves throughout Africa, Madagascar, and Australia.

I say these things, draw attention to these earth-bound teachers, because these things matter—because all the worlds, large and miniature; all the plants, animals, landscapes, and bodies, and all the teachings and wisdoms they speak, matter because they *are matter*. All the world, and all the things and beings it bears, are manifestations of the God-particle—consisting matter of the cosmos. All the stuff of creation, all the plants, animals, fishes, reptiles, birds, and insects; all the rivers, streams, lakes, and dried river beds, all the oceans and deserts; all the fossils, rocks, and minerals—all the atom-made, compound-consisting elements of our little blue planet and the entire cosmos—speak to the unbridled, sheer, and breathtaking presence of life and all its diversity. Moreover, all that is speaks. All that is proclaims the germinal, life-birthing Grove-ground of originations.

And yet, despite the many earth-bound voices speaking a multiplicity of holy cosmic languages, telling us of a diversity-loving natural order, teaching us all the marvelous ways life embodies beautifully mysterious forms, the fearful framers of Creationism fail to comprehend the basic truths proclaimed by the totality—and the particularities—of the very same creation in which they claim to take a stand. They fail to apprehend and understand the foundational reality known to the earth, itself, and to all of us who are able to recall our Grove beginnings. That is, in a world where there are more than ten thousand species of grasses, providing homes to eleven thousand known species of grasshoppers, all growing under, around, or near more than sixty thousand species of trees which, in turn, are homes to more than ten thousand species of birds, it is simply *not* possible that there are *only* two forms of human beings. In fact, it is preposterous.

The truth is, much to the discomfort of narrow fundamentalism, nature, too, is abundant with agender beings, sex-changing beings, and a host of living plants and animals that reproduce parthenogenetically. That is, there are plants and invertebrate animals that reproduce through production of unfertilized eggs. Thus, the idea that even these miraculous creatures I am discussing naturally develop into *only* "male" and "female" forms is equally preposterous. In fact, across species, trees manifest a range of genders and many—such as maples and yews—are capable of changing their sex as well as their behavior, appearance, or gender. Additionally, clownfish and other fishes change their sex, including reproductive behavior, as a normal process. Some, like moray eels, are more non-binary and display both male and female designated eel-traits, visibly and equally. In all of nature, as with human beings, there is a naturally occurring multitude of sex and gender possibilities.

In all their efforts to subjugate and subdue the earth, God-fearing fundamentalists fail to speak to the earth. Therefore, they fail to learn from it. They fail to see the Grove for the trees around it. Thus, they fail to recognize that trees are more than trunks with roots and branches—that their roots go deep and form networks, like neurons, through which they communicate information, share nutrients, disperse disease and predation-preventing substances, and even nourish the aging stumps of felled trees with sugar solutions. They have forgotten that trees are time-keepers and living libraries of history. Makers of constructs seem to fear the knowledge trees hold and carry, seem to fear the wisdom of grasshoppers, humming-birds, and snakes. Even as they proclaim creation, box-making fundamentalists fail to listen to the truths creation speaks with many voices and, thus, they fail to hear, and heed, all the bare and beautiful Grove-proclaiming wisdom the things and beings of the earth are ever-singing.

Because they cannot grasp the reality of the Grove for all the branch-bearing trees and ground-sustaining grasses along its borders, they also cannot comprehend, more meaningfully, all the boundary-dwelling, threshold-crossing beings born in the life-giving ground of the embryonic Grove. Because, in the world of constructs, trees are simply trees, the makers of absolutes cannot recognize all the many ways our boundary-dwelling kindred slip the false skins of codifications, make transit across classifications, and cross the thresholds of narrow expectations. As such, the Grove-born surviv-al intelligence of hummingbird moths is lost to the fundamentalist world. That they fly like hummingbirds rather than moths, vibrate so intensely they appear not to move at all as they hover over blossoms, and move through the air with graceful speed testifies trans-dimensional power and wisdom. Like gender-transcendent persons, they transgress simplistic expectations and presumed permissibilities of being.

Similarly, our other relations are lost at the boundaries of Grove and world. Our marvelously intelligent, adaptive trans-dimensional kindred are everywhere. The proclamations they speak, like our gender-transcendent testimonies, announce and attest to the ongoing, ever-emerging divine imaginary in which axolotls and platypuses, too, are our kindred.

An axolotl, unlike other salamanders, retains its dorsal fin—rather like a tadpole—as well as the somewhat feathery gills from its larval beginnings. Additionally, axolotls seldom transition to being land creatures. They live their lives in the water; thus, they are often called "walking fish." Found exclusively in the Xochimilco lake complexes near Mexico City, axolotls are now an endangered species—rather like us. Similarly, the being of a platypus resists the narrow confines of human codification and classifications. The platypus lives, largely, on land near the waters in Australia, but it hunts and feeds underwater. They are not beavers, but have a beaver-like tail. Nor are they otters, though they have fur like otters and a similar body. Like ducks, platypuses have webbed feet and bills. They are neither ducks nor beavers nor otters. A platypus is, decidedly, something more. Like hummingbird moths, axolotls, and many other creatures, platypuses are codification-resisting, threshold-crossing kindred of a kind. They challenge the simplistic categories that humans like to apply to them.

All these earth-bound beings speak. Their presence, their living-on, tells stories of a vast, generations-long memory of the Primal Grove. The Grove—all its elements, materials, compounds, creatures, and beings—speaks through all that is now, ever was, and ever will be. All of creation, including us, voices sacred syllables, singing hymns to the natural necessity of diverse differentiation. If we speak to the earth, utter inquiries to earth-born beings, we will gleen liberating, world-transforming truths. The miraculous beings of hummingbird moths, baobab trees, axolotls, and platypuses, like all the earth—and most surely, like all gender- transcendent persons—speak the continually unfolding living text of the divine imaginary, which is not bound by or to human forms, ideas, or rules. In a universe where baobab trees, axolotls, hummingbirds, and hummingbird moths exist, it is simply impossible that there should be, or must be, only two forms of human beings—whatever those presumed binary ways of being might be. The Grove, and each of us, tells these truths.

Long ago, Grandmother taught me that people are like geodes. Not only are no two the same, one never knows how beautiful they are or of what marvelous forces and elements they are made, until something breaks them open. This, I am sure, is gender-transcendent knowledge, born and carried in our bodies, in our fleshy-geode skin, bone, and blood. For who we are to be revealed, for all that is within us to shine, sparkling, glinting in the sun—in diverse, individuated ways—we break ourselves open. That shimmery, stunning light is simply, and sadly, too much for some to bear.

chapter ten

Completing the Circle:
Returning to the Grove

... may it be my custom to go outdoors each day
among the trees and grass,
among all the growing things,
and there may I be alone,
and enter into prayer ...
Nachman of Breslov (1772–1810)
Hasidic Rabbi
from "A Final Prayer"

The ideal is for a person to be a revelation oneself—
clearly to recognize oneself as a manifestation of God.
Baal Shem Tov (1698–1760)
Founder of Hasidic Judaism

As troubling as we and all the glorious truths we bear seem to be to lovers of neat and orderly, fearfully unimaginative binary assumptions, we exist nonetheless. And, we shine. Like splashes of sun on dew-drenched leaves and grasses along the winding path back to the Grove, we shimmer beautiful dreams of living on, of becoming. The Creator-God calls all things into being and delights in the unfolding richness of it all. The fact that so many people are unable to dream Eden-recalling, life-budding dreams alongside us in no way diminishes or erases all of the revelations and wisdoms our living on in daring audacity proclaims. So, too, the inability of so many to follow us, perhaps joyfully, back to the germinal Grove in no way diminishes the facts of our lives. Nor does it diminish the facts of the barely perceptible, sun-soaked Grove within us, as surely as we are, ever, in it.

Grandmother's wisdom is strong. Persistent. Not only in our gender-transcendent bodies and the bodies of geodes, but in the body of the world as well. To recognize and then to apprehend the beauty and testimonies of the world of beings and things, we have to break open the layers of false-skin assumptions, shed the constrictive confines of codifications, and loose the world that *is* from the world that is not—freeing all that matters from the thought-worlds of constructed anti-matter. This is true not only of the living testimony-texts of bodies and world, but it is also profoundly true of the texts of scripture.

All these observations and ponderings—indeed, all the proclamations posed in this project of Trans-Forming Proclamation—return us to the beginning—not only to the Sacred Grove, itself, but also to the misread Creator-experiencing thoughts, stories, and proclamations of our ancestors. All our returning leads back to the one, Holy Other, and to this Creator-God's divine imaginary. Specifically, the proposed proclamations in this project journey back to the idea that the Holy Other created earthly humans in "the Image of God"—and the proposition that the misreading of that image is the first cause of so many of our various oppressions as gender-transcendent persons.

For centuries, especially in the cherished, hallowed halls of Christendom, the statement in Genesis 1:27 has been misread. So persistently so, in fact, that the misreading itself has become a gospel of a kind, covering even supposed scholarly readings of the Hebrew among Christian theologians, professors, and preachers. Human bias works like this: sometimes the accepted, traditional presumption speaks with such vehemence that the letters on the page are lost. This kind of reverent worshiping of contrived absolute interpretations is the root cause of our oppressions—including not only oppression based on sex and gender, but also those based on race, class, and the supporting codifications they produce.

Christian theology, traditionally, has read Genesis 1:27 to say this: "God created *man* in *His* own image; in *the* image of God, *He* created *him*." From this reading, one fundamental, overarching, and absolute image of humans—and therefore, of the Holy Otherness we call God—has been assumed, prescribed, and applied to denote and govern what it means to be a normal, naturally occurring human being, and who is and is not a normative human being. The misreading of this text has served to denote which human forms have ultimate value over others. Through centuries of various, increasingly sophisticated descriptions of human beings, forged into standards, expectations, and dehumanizing value systems, we know exactly what this human looks like and who is represented by it. And, we know who is left out, cast-out, debased, and devalued by its rendering.

However, a more searching and robust reading of the Hebrew clarifies this, in fact, is *not* what the text says. Before I detail the most powerful personhood-affirming truth in the language of this verse, I want to reveal another layer to the gendered nature of Hebrew. While it is true that some words have gendered forms and the default for many forms is often masculine, it is also true that, in Hebrew, the gendered rendering can also be read as the gender-neutral article, "it." So, where the text refers to God in masculinized forms, the text can also be read as implying a neutral, *it*, or *itself*—perhaps, even, a person-centred neutral, *they*, *them*, or *themself*. That said, the Grove-remembering, selfhood-validating implications are significant. Firstly, as I have iterated at length, the Hebrew word phrase does not say precisely God made "man" in God's image. The text says God made the being made from the ground of the earth: the *adam*. Secondly, more pointedly, is a truth found in the word phrase, in Genesis 1:27, toward which the whole project of this book ultimately points.

The word phrase commonly translated as "in *the* image of God," is actually rendered to reveal that a more proper reading is that the earth-being, *ha-adam*, was made "in God's image," or in "*an* image of God." For those unfamiliar with the process of translation, I want to stress that nuances in meaning are lost, or at least obscured, when the words are moved out of their thought-world habitat and thrust into another language. Translation is, itself, an act of interpretation, as words can mean more than one thing and can be used in multiple ways in any language; thus, bias has a natural point of entry into the process. As I have proposed, bias itself is an unavoidable reality of being enculturated by societies, histories, personal contexts, learning, and experiences. It is also somewhat neutral. The tasks are to become aware of them, own them, and where biases get in the way of exercising our meaning-making abilities, to work through them. In the case of this single Genesis verse, bias has been formed by the "rules" of English linguistics (applied to Hebrew), literalist semantics, and the prescriptions of a patriarchal, cisgender, dominant culture.

In English, possession is indicated by the use of an apostrophe, usually followed by an "s." In Hebrew, to indicate possessiveness—that is, to say that something is *of*, or *belongs to* something or someone else—the language makes use of a form called a "construct phrase." Construct phrases in Hebrew do not contain any articles, definite or otherwise (a, an, the). Translating these phrases into English requires addition of an article so the meaning makes sense in English. In some cases, readers often *assume* grammatical definiteness, which means that something is *the* singular, defined and specific—and sometimes, *only*—thing of something or someone else. Enculturation in English grammar leads to assuming this particular Hebrew construct phrase denotes definiteness and, therefore, requires the definite article, "the," to indicate a singular, model image of God.

But, Hebrew does not function that way. Construct phrases in Hebrew are more about *determining* that something distinct and particular *belongs* to something or someone else. Thus, the particular something is, primarily, *a* something, not *the* something. For example, when talking about the moon belonging to our earth, we would say, "*the* earth's moon," because there is only one. Thus, our article, "the," is both definite and determinative. However, of a person's book left on a desk, we would say, "someone's book" (*a* book belonging to someone) because it surely is not the only book in the world—nor is it likely to be the only book someone has. Therefore, the implied article is "a," not "the," because the object is not definite. It is only determined to belong to someone.

That said, in the thought-world of Hebrew, the phrase tradition-ally read to say "*the* image of God," means *an* image *belonging* to God and the character of that image was God's own image. So, the text determines possessiveness—that is, an image *of* God, an image God has. This image, then, was made particular, distinct, and set apart in a specific earth-made human being. The phrase does not say that God made *ha-adam* in the specific, singular, and therefore, *only* image of God. The construct phrase, *b'tselem Elohim*, reads, simply: in [*an*] image of God. That is, in God's image.

Equally significant, the word *Elohim* is, itself, a plural form re-ferring to God. Depending on context, *elohim* can mean "gods," more generally, as in the gods of other lands and peoples. When context clearly refers to the monotheistic idea of an Existing One, it means simply, God—a pluralistic term, functioning in the singular. Giv-en this odd plurality, then, Genesis 1:26 actually reads: let *Us* make *ha-adam* in *Our* (pluralistic) *image*, according to *Our likeness*. To em-phasize the depth of the phrase (and indeed, the proclamations in this work), *Elohim* could be read to refer to, and denote, a Holy Other who is a unity—that is, a unified oneness—of multiple qualities, at-tributes, expressions, disclosures, and images.

To be sure, the depth, totality, and multiplicity of these qualities, attributes, expressions, disclosures, and images are most decidedly beyond us. Therefore, we do not know—and cannot know—a full apprehension of what images, presentations, and features constitute an image of God's selfhood. All we have before us are the storied imaginings of our ancestors, a grouping of their written expres-sions, and our experiences of those stories, ourselves, one another, our world, and perhaps God. From these, together, we can discern that there are as many *images* of God as there are now, ever have been, or ever will be earth-stuff humans. What is equally sure is that our scripture-writing ancestors possessed a worldview that proposed we human beings—in our multiplicity of distinct, individuated, and conspicuous personhood-containing habitations—were conceived of and born into a sacred divine imaginary that, by God-particle consisting nature, is not bound by, or subject to, human constructs of absolute forms.

And so, it is. The mythological constructs of the universal human, by which we are measured, over and over, across all manner of partial histories and constrictive dictates, is broken open for us to recognize. And, resist. And, refute. The text is like a big, heavy mud-and-gunk-covered geode, buried and obscured long ago by power-keepers who hoped it would never be found—that it would never be broken-open, laying bare all the world-transforming, diversity-affirming power that gleams crystalline, truth-revealing light within it. Gazing into the sun-drenched light splattering and shimmering on all the truth that lies within, far beneath the false-skin layers of human unimagining, we can see the Grove. It is there—winking an axolotl-salamander wink, stretching baobab branches, and flapping sheer, quick, hummingbird moth wings.

And we remember. We belong here. We are valuable still-speaking, sameness-resisting, differentiated living-on remnants of *Something More.* We matter because we *are* matter—God-particle consisting, sacred otherness-proclaiming, set-apart beings of the Sacred Grove.

Here, in the bare fullness of all that is now, ever was, and ever will be, on this holy ground, we can take off our shoes, slip the skins of an ill-fitting world, and push ourselves into a warm patch of soft grass and breathe. Here, in the stillness of the life-giving Grove, we can take our place as borderland threshold-crossing beings of the divine imaginary. And, like all the life within the Sacred Grove— sometimes in whispers, sometimes in shouts and songs, sometimes in simply living on—we can speak our heartfelt, experience-born, trans-formational proclamations.

chapter eleven

Trans-Forming Proclamation

The spirit of the Sovereign is upon me
for the Everlasting has anointed me;
God has sent me as a herald of joy to the afflicted,
to bind up the wounded of heart,
to proclaim liberty to the captives
and the opening of the prison to those who are bound;
to proclaim a year of God's favor and a day of
vindication by our God—to comfort all who mourn.

Isaiah 61:1-2
author's translation

Like the Grove that bears our footprints, living on speaks;
sacred syllables burst forth from our daring to be and become ourselves.
In the daily miracles of our lives, holy secrets are
revealed. We are invited and called, each in our ways of being, to
notice, claim and proclaim the signs of Holiness imaged,
present, and discernable in the differentiated particularity in all of
creation, entire. Even, and perhaps especially, us.

Excerpt, Chapter Four: Sacred Grove, Living Proclamation

The Sacred Grove is ever-speaking—in all its manifestations and iter-ations; across time and the march of human histories, known and obscured, nearly erased and still remembered; the Grove speaks. So, too, do we as gender-transcendent, particular persons. In all our liv-ing-on, in all our borderland-dwelling, threshold-crossing, codification-transgressing bodies, our daring existence testifies. We have stories to tell. Sacred syllables burst forth in the stories of our lives—those we choose to speak; those we choose to carry in silence; those we choose to utter through the brilliant, daily light of our bodies, bold and present in the living of our days. Like the Grove, itself, we testify. Sometimes, in whispers; sometimes, in crying out; sometimes, in exclamations of joy; sometimes in silence; and, sometimes, in song, our very presence speaks proclamations of the Eden-recalling, diversity-declaring, endlessly unfolding Divine Imaginary of beings, forces, and things.

Broadly speaking, Trans-Forming Proclamation is many things and performs several distinct tasks. **Trans-Forming Proclamation is an expression of diverse, gender-transcendent embodiments daring to live on in an ill-fitting world that wishes we did not exist, a world that fears us and all the paradigm-upending messages we embody.** The act of daring to boldly and bravely live on, to exist in equally diverse and personal ways, makes it possible to become intentional about drawing on and allowing our lives to speak the knowledge-ways, wisdoms, and insights we carry.

Thus, Trans-Forming Proclamation is a *methodology*—a way of thinking, being, and doing in a world of ill-fitting, troubling constructs. By this, I mean Trans-Forming Proclamation is a kind of active *theory*: an applied set of values and systems of ideas employed to propose informed assumptions, offer affirmations and declarations, make truth-claims and, often, proclaim faith-claims. Thus, it is a way of going about thinking in particular ways and applying ideas, engaging imagination, shedding ill-fitting ideas, messages, and imposed ways of being. It is, always, a magical, life-giving process of conjuring new ways of thinking, doing, and being.

At the core, this active methodology—this way of *being, thinking, and doing*—is a reflective praxis. It is a process that relies upon and employs our deepest imagination and our multivalent ways of calling vital images, knowledge-ways, life-ways, and means of creating new things into being. That is, Trans-Forming Proclamation is also a *way of enacting and embodying* the truths of our existence: a particular way of doing reflective inquiry and making embodied proclamations—as well as a way of living our daily lives. In essence, Trans-Forming Proclamation is the practice of engaging experience, scripture, story, history, circumstances, and world through our gender-diverse identities. We form truth-claims and faith-propositions about ourselves and about the God we discover experientially, while expressing these claims in our daily living, meaning-making, speaking, creating, and especially, daring existence.

Throughout this project, I have stated that Trans-Forming Proclamation assumes and asserts that we, as gender-transcendent persons largely cast out of communities of faith and often deeply harmed by them, possess—and are justified in claiming—the right to seek after the God who abides with and speaks to us. At the very least, we have the same right as anyone else to engage all our longing, curiosity, and hope for God by seeking deeper, more meaningful connection to the God *we perceive and experience*—and to do so using all the knowledge-ways, wisdom-ways, and ways of understanding we may be able to access in order to cultivate and nurture meaningful relationship with Holy Presence, ourselves, others, and our world.

The practice of Trans-Forming Proclamation is one way of seeking possible answers. Essential to such a pursuit, to the project of personal faith formation and development, are the primary questions of who God is, or might be; what might be the nature of this God; what is the nature of our experience of God; what are claims we can make, experientially and through all our ways of knowing, about how God acts, or does not, in our lives, earthly conditions, and our world; and in what ways do our relations with others affect and contribute to these experiences?

To lift up a metaphor: to engage Trans-Forming Proclamation is to cross the threshold of gender-transcendent abiding, move into the Sacred Grove of perennial beingness—returning, again, to ourselves and our *other-space* origins—and, there, settle our tender selves onto the fecund earth, renewing our sense of self and our connection with the God of the Grove and our own understanding. It is to center into our bodies, look and listen to all that is within us and around us, with our senses, intelligences, knowledges, and intuitions, attending to the God who comes to us everywhere. It is to make declarations of what we find, discern, and experience in that other-space, and in the texts of world, circumstances, relationships, and scripture.

This centering into our bodies is profoundly important because our bodies matter—because our bodies *are* matter, the individuated, particularity-infused, Grove-recalling particles of God. Our embodied living on proclaims the sovereignty of the body as place; of individual, selfhood-endowed belonging in body and in all of creation. We carry in our blood, bone, and skin not only the history of the Sacred Grove and all our threshold-crossing relations, across time and space, but also of our ancestors, the histories of seemingly endless oppressions, and our own personal wisdom-making histories. Our bodies remember all that the ill-fitting world hopes will be forgotten. Our enspirited bodies bear stories, knowledge, and wisdoms unique to us and profoundly important to the reimagining of the world we inhabit, dreaming, and conjuring something new. Our bodied living on speaks. Our bodies testify, teach, resist, remember, imagine, and proclaim the many trans-formational truths carried in the primeval body of the Grove. In our miraculous, magical, boundary-dwelling bodies we embody the Eden-recalling Grove. And, together, we speak.

To do trans-formed proclamation is to acknowledge, affirm, and claim our position in that holy *gender-other-space* and to proclaim our relational connections to the God of the hidden, outcast Grove—the germinal world we inhabit—to other persons, and to our own experiences. It is to claim our place in the divine imaginary of beings, to declare our necessity to the world we inhabit, to renew our place in the whole of the still-being-written story of humanity, and, most assuredly, to bring a deeper, more meaningful shared understanding of what it means to be a human being in relationship with other humans—and, perhaps, God.

To turn a classically Christian phrase, this proclamation that our presence contributes to the ongoing, collective human discernment of what it means to be a person is Good News. It is a gospel proclaiming that ongoing, participatory trans-formation is *essential* to being a human being seeking authentic personhood, growth, and personal development, self-expression, purposeful contribution, relational connection, and sense of place and belonging—and, perhaps, some sense of God. It is Good News to all who seek after justice, for as sacred human worlds in miniature, we proclaim much pertaining to the ways and means that either destroy or preserve a life. This living testimony is not only good news for gender-transcendent persons longing to be at home in body, in world, and in community, but profoundly good news to every human person who longs for a more felt freedom to live and move and have their being within a deeper sense of self, of belonging and of connection to others, to all that is, and possibly, especially to the Oneness we call God.

In the remainder of this closing chapter, I will attempt to address certain questions of a less poetic nature. What do I mean by proclamation? What do I mean by trans-forming? What are the essential assumptions of Trans-Forming Proclamation? And, how do we practice Trans-Forming Proclamation?

What Is Proclamation?

In general terms, to make a proclamation is to announce something. The act of proclamation, more specifically, is the assertive statement of a certain claim made in speech, in writing, or in demonstration; it is an affirmational profession of the truth, reality, and/or validity of something both particular and significant. Merriam Webster defines the verb *proclaim* as meaning: "to declare publicly, typically insistently, proudly, or defiantly and in either speech or writing; or, to give outward indication of" something. A proclamation is filled with words that matter (even more than usual). Not just words of observation, or of theories removed from practices, but words that invite the lessons of Grove into being—words that conjure its image before us, that we might apprehend it, so we might manifest its wisdoms anew, everywhere we are.

The methodology of Trans-Forming Proclamation begins with a belief that there are many ways of making and speaking sacred declarations. From there, a primary assumption is that gender-tran-

117

scendent persons, through both our nature and presence in the world of creation, are capable of making particular kinds of proclamation. Gender-transcendent proclamations matter, not just for individual meaning-making and expression of authenticity, but also because of what they tell us about the world, about God, about our relationships, about our bodies, and about how we know anything (and everything).

In this work, I am proposing a distinct and specific form and process of proclamation: a Trans-Forming Proclamation. Trans-*formed* proclamation comes from within our embodied selves, our enspirited bodies; its endeavors emerge within and arise from *our* experiences of selfhood in body, in the world, and in our own discernment. Trans-*formed* proclamation is the product of our process—the revelation from *our* searching, *our* questioning investigations, *our* learning, wisdom, and proposition-making. So, trans-formed proclamation relies defiantly on truth-claims born of our lived experience, even—and especially—when that lived experience, when the knowledge that comes from within, contradicts external signifiers such as culture or tradition.

Even as our endeavors to become more fully authentic, relational selves require and involve—perhaps, demand—a willingness to be both vulnerable and fearless, open and protectively guarded, conspicuous and inconspicuous, boldly visible and safety-seeking, revealing our proclamations equally carries the same paradoxes and tensions. These realities, in fact, shape the power of our testimonies. Trans-Forming Proclamation is an ever-evolving process of vulnerable, brave, ongoing discernment of *what* to reveal, what to keep close to us; *how* to disclose revelations, to *whom*, and under what circumstances. Each of us must make those decisions, in each situation, through our own discernment. Because all of our proclamations are *formed* and *informed* by our gender-transcendent and other identities, our wisdom is deep, far-reaching, and full of world-changing insights and practices.

However, it is also true that an abundance of our knowledge-ways can be shared without specifically disclosing our status as gender-transcendent persons. Sometimes, the Grove remains hidden behind a veil, yet retains all the power of creation nonetheless. These choices are personal and we carry within us, in our very bodies, the wisdom and discernment to make the choices we need to make. No one else can do so on our behalf. Claiming and taking our place in that power are also, paradoxically, expressions of our living proclamation.

That is, by living on, we proclaim the Grove, all the elements and forces and beings of life within it, and most surely the Creator-God who indwells both the Grove and each of us. When we honor and regard ourselves, when we respect and tend our bodies, when we care for ourselves and treat ourselves as well as we are able, when we do whatever we must do to preserve our lives and our selves, we equally honor, respect, tend, care for, and preserve the Grove. These practices teach us and make us more able to be in sacred relationships with others. In so doing, we honor, regard, and express the God of the Grove. Daring to exist, resistantly refusing to collapse under the weights of an ill-fitting world gone far astray of the Grove, is a powerful proclamation. Often, it is a proclamation that never needs to be spoken because the light that shines forth from such a life is breathtaking, illuminating everything around us.

Christian Preaching vs. Prophetic Proclamation

It is important to acknowledge that the idea of "proclamation," increasingly in modernity, has been associated almost solely with Christian preaching paradigms. Therefore, when the term *proclamation* is used, it is perceived as referring to—and privileging—Christian preaching tropes and traditions. I want to be clear that I am diverging from that expectation. In fact, I am employing and trans-forming an older paradigm, one that actually took on a particular form and expression with the Hebrew prophets.

The prophets, in their self-understanding and discernment of call and vocation, employed, transformed, and moved beyond words. It could be said, they invented a kind of lived performance proclamation. The prophets did whatever was necessary, even with their bodies, to express the message of liberating justice they discerned was given to them. In fact, their prophecy was not about fortune-telling; it was about truth-telling—exposing the injustices and inhumanities of their times and proclaiming a vision of just repair and renewal. They understood that words matter because words *are* matter, that the thought-worlds of words can be put to tearing down or to build-ing-up a more just, equitable, compassionate world.

The prophets, indeed, spoke truth as it was given to them in their understanding. They also went to unusual extremes to make their points. Though we cannot reasonably assume that these prophets were gender-transcendent kindred (though some may have been), we can draw parallels to the many ways we, through expressions of our bodiedness, our actions, and our lives, make emphatic, liberative proclamations.

As surely as we make alterations to the ways in which we dress, choosing clothing more suitable to us, and wear our clothing in unique ways that make statements about who we are, the prophets did the same to proclaim their messages. Isaiah, for example, stripped off his clothes and went around completely naked (Isaiah 20). Jere-miah, we are told, hid his undergarments under a rock, for a long period of time, and then went back to retrieve them (Jeremiah 13). Afterward, he fastened a cattle yoke around his shoulders and wore it (Jeremiah 27–28). In addition to these embodiments of prophetic statements, not too dissimilar from our own, the prophets engaged in behaviors and modes of self-expression outside of "respectable" norms. Similar to the ways in which many among us alter our bodies to speak more authentically who we are, they were fully prepared to devote even the use of their bodies to a message they believed to be bigger than and beyond themselves.

Hosea married a sex worker to iterate the message that the peo-ple were engaging in spiritual adultery against God—worshiping false gods, committing idolatry, and forsaking the commandments. He and Gomer, his sex-worker spouse, had children together. Be-cause words matter, God instructed Hosea to give them names that conveyed prophetic messages: *Lo'ammi*, meaning "not my people"; *Jezreel*, meaning "God will sow"; and *Lo'ruchamah*, meaning "without compassion," or "no compassion." Ezekiel, who was initially rendered mute, made drawings on clay tablets, portraying Jerusalem under siege. Then, as God instructed him, he placed an iron pan between himself and his drawing and lay down on his side on the ground with the pan and his art. For the sins of Israel, he lay on his side for 390 days; then, he turned over on his right side to bear the sins of Judah for 40 days—one day to symbolize a year (Ezekiel 4). The story tells us that Ezekiel even consented to being tied and bound with ropes—by none other than God—so that he could not turn over until the appointed time.

Later, in another marvelously burlesque form of ancient Near Eastern performance art, Ezekiel used a sword to cut off his beard (Ezekiel 5). Then, he weighed his beard, and divided it into thirds. One third, he burned in the city when the siege was over; a second third, he chopped up and spread on the ground as he moved around the city; and the final third, he scattered to the winds. He held out a few strands, kept them in his clothes until an appointed time, and then burned those too. All of this he did to draw attention to the ways the people had strayed from the path and, in so doing, brought tribulation upon themselves.

There is much more that could be said about all of these stories. For our purposes, the point is that they engaged in certain behaviors and comported themselves in particular ways—often odd, strange, unusual, and, dare I say, queer ways. They did things with their clothing, including their hair, ate particular foods, took long journeys, and often performed miracles. Frequently, they did so in extreme, oddly unusual, even burlesque, performative ways. Their goals were rooted in truth-telling the realities afflicting the people in their here-and-now. They were offering an alternative vision for communal liberation, conjuring an earthly society that foreshadowed the holy community of the world to come.

Their messages were not aimed at creating in others an intellectual belief in a Divine Being. The presence of God in the cosmic order and the world was assumed. The questions the prophets sought to answer were about how we ought to comport ourselves *with one an-*

other in a world where God exists in relationship with all of creation. They understood that revelations about how we might live together more compassionately and justly require a *living* proclamation.

I do not say this to digress. The point is important. I want to distinguish Trans-Forming Proclamation from considerations associated merely, or only, with Christian preaching tropes. It is much bigger and broader—and perhaps, more ancient—than that. Where Christian preaching is frequently concerned with the nature of, and acceptance into, an afterlife, Trans-Forming Proclamation is concerned with the conditions of our lives in *our* here-and-now. Like the prophets before us, Trans-Forming Proclamation is concerned with the systemic, institutional, and structural sins that serve to create outcasts, strangers, widows, orphans, and other disregarded, forgotten people—precisely because we, too, are their people and they are ours.

Trans-Forming Proclamation is less concerned with proof-texting the existence of God and more concerned with discovering, through all our seeking and means of knowing, ways that our presence in the world, individually and collectively, can inform and assist in creating ways of earthly cohabitation consistent with a cosmos in which the presence of God is assumed. Trans-Forming Proclamation is not at all concerned with creating converts and saving eternal souls; it is concerned with discovering and creating ideas, practices, and policies for saving our lives—likely, the lives of other *othered* peoples, and quite possibly our world. Like the strange, queer, and performative prophets of old, Trans-Forming Proclamation is concerned with truth-telling, from the powerful testimonies of our lives, from all our seeking and discovery, and from the wisdom of our individual and common experiences in a dominating world, ill-suited to the fullfilment of human longing.

As a people born into the primordial Grove, we are as ancient as the original *adam*. Generation after generation, we testify to the vast, ever-unfolding diversity of human potentialities—embodied life after embodied life, proclamation after proclamation. Trans-Forming Proclamation is embodied, lived and living, and seeks to consist ways of being authentic selves within discernment of the experiences, values, principles, and practices inherent in what is proclaimed. Therefore, in the active search for congruent authenticity in our bodies and in the world, the living presence of gender-transcendent persons constitutes a living, trans-*formed* proclamation. This collective reality simply *is*, even as it can also be made more intentional and more purposeful in multiple and diverse ways—all of which surely point to liberation and justice.

What is Trans-Forming?

Trans-Forming Proclamation emerges within and from *trans-formed* and *in-formed* persons. What I mean to say is: Trans-Forming Proclamation arises from within persons who are gender-transcendent persons—that is, from those of us formed in and by transgender, nonbinary, gender non-conforming, and/or intersex experiences; those of us whose personhoods, lives, experiences, knowledge, insights, and wisdom are shaped, informed, and formed by being gender-transcendent persons. That is, by being people who have been pressed to conform, pressed to deny ourselves, and ultimately, pressed to transform ourselves—to slip false-skins, and reveal ourselves, even if only to ourselves and those closest to us.

Being trans is not something we do once and it is done. It is a life-way, in its own right. Being gender-transcendent in a world that only thinks narrowly of gender is a lifestance. My use of the term "trans-forming" points to the reality that ours is a proclamation that is always in and informed by *process*; this is so because we exist, always, in states of ongoing, evolving, self-discerning and self-revealing processes of becoming, but also because our very existence, even as it evolves, exists in opposition to the ill-fitting skin of the world of un-imagining.

Therefore, a true and meaningful Trans-Forming Proclamation cannot and does not come from those whose embodied formations and experiences align neatly with the prescribed, reductive, and oppressive gender or sex binaries, no matter how well-intended their desires to speak for and about us might be. Other marginalized experiences offer their own insights. While others can learn from our particular expressions of Trans-Forming Proclamation; while they may perhaps find inspiration for their own allyship-seeking assertions of trans-*affirming* proclamations, persons who are not-us simply cannot make actual Trans-Forming Proclamations. Trans-Forming Proclamation, as process and practice, assumes origination in some gender-transcendent state of being.

It is important to reiterate a point made early on in this proclamation project. Being a gender-transcendent person is, itself, a paradox of personhood. That is, gender-transcendence is not born within the kind of essentialism we have been conditioned to believe is rigid, fixed, and pre-ordained. Who any of us are, as individual persons, is an ongoing, evolving expression of endowed selfhood arising and taking shape through a continual unfolding of dispositions, characteristics, and traits shaped and formed through experiences, relationships, and encounters experienced in the world of other people and human-made constructs. Said another way, we are—all of us—Grove-born, selfhood-endowed persons continually shaped and formed by socializations and enculturations.

Yet, some magical sense of selfhood pre-exists socialization in a mysterious way. Otherwise, we could not *know* that who we *are* is not who the world, at large, tells us we are or can be. Were it not for the contrived codifications imposed upon our sense of self by constructed ideologies of permissible and normative ways of being persons, we would be simply persons who manifest a sense of self defined and made conspicuous to others by different factors, characteristics, and features. But, we do not live in such a world. Therefore, we are particularly formed and shaped by gender-transcendent experiences, self-understandings, and relationalities. We are forced by imposed personhood prescriptions to think about ourselves, talk about, transform, and reveal ourselves in terms of gender-transcendence. In equally paradoxical ways, then, the creation of strict gender classifications is a response to us—throughout history—to which we, then, are forced to respond in our search for a meaningful, and liveable, sense of self. We are *made* other and the construct of that otherness is gender-transcendence.

Further, to exist in a gender-transcendent state of being is to be displaced from a valued and participatory sense of communal place in the mainstream world—a world we both inhabit and are shunned from fully entering, a world from which we are marginalized. Gender-transcendent persons live, every day, in various states of dislocation based not only on the sociopolitical constructs of gender, but also and especially upon the constructs of race, class, national origin, ethnicity, and ability, in addition to other interlocking identities. Because the world of narrow human constructs has, also, actively displaced the primordial Grove, we whose very existence recalls and remembers that germinal space are also dislocated from our own internal awareness and proclamation of it. We are forced to search and grope for it, within and among ourselves, through our own intuitions of its spectral presence, and to call it into being through creation of our own sanctuary spaces and places.

Therefore, those whose identities afford them meaningful measures of participation in the rights, resources, protections, and current privileges of the larger society simply cannot create the Trans-Forming Proclamations we speak into the world. While others may hold valuable wisdoms that affect or impact a robust Trans-Forming Proclamation, while some may possess lived experiences that connect with other layers of gender-transcendent oppressions, a truly Trans-Forming Proclamation arises within the complex, socially stratified experiences of gender-transcendent persons.

That said, Trans-Forming Proclamation crosses paths and holds dialogic relationships with important theological journey-ways that push against, refute, and reimagine traditional theologies—particularly Christian, as well as more conservative non-Christian theologies. However, by working to deconstruct faulty, harmful assumptions within the gender binary, Trans-Forming Proclamation addresses concerns generally left out of theology, continues where others move off the path, and corrects exclusionary logic errors permeating the bulk of purportedly progressive, or even radical, theological methodologies. In these ways, our work recenters theological searching and thought in bodied experiences of the most basic and fundamental aspects of what it is to be a human person and then approaches study, reflection, and interpretation from such positioning.

Where white feminist theology takes the positions that there is no superior gender, no single universal form of womanhood, and yet that there are prescribed features that create womanhood, the theory gets lost in the weeds of essentialism. It attempts to define what these essential features are and are not—and thus undermines its own argument by failing to accept trans women and generally ignoring non-binary persons, intersex persons, as well as radically, high-femme–identified persons. In the extreme, trans-exclusionary radical feminists become the very sex-gender oppressors from which they claim to free themselves. Trans-Forming Proclamation begins with correcting these false assumptions by rejecting gender and sex essentialism and arguing for a continual reimagining of both gender and sex, recognizing and celebrating an infinite multitude of gender, sex, and sexuality possibilities and potentialities.

Where mainstream queer theology undermines its own discourse through yet another sexuality-based binary, by pink-washing sex and gender in the assumption that gender-transcendence is some form of extreme sexuality—or *gayness*—Trans-Forming Proclamation frees sex, gender, bodiedness, and sexuality from the confines of essentialist dictates and the assumption that sexuality is fixed in any expression. It could be said, Trans-Forming Proclamation transcends queer theology and pushes it to the logical positions to which it already points, but generally fails to apprehend.

By beginning our process with the assumptions that the possession, self-understanding, and expression of gender are fundamental to personhood, and that personhood, itself, constitutes a set of potentialities endowed within us and is, therefore, beyond the proscriptions of socioculturally constructed absolutes, Trans-Forming Proclamation is uniquely positioned to name, analyze, and interrogate intersectional power and identity-based oppressions. In fact, Trans-Forming Proclamation assumes that gender-transcendent persons are uniquely, and particularly, targeted and harmfully affected by intersectional power. As such, a trans-forming methodology exists within and claims places of power and proclamation at the margins of oppressive margins. Trans-Forming Proclamation recognizes kinship with liberation theologies and then, beginning with the questions and concerns of gender, moves transgressively farther by seeking to apprehend the layered, intersecting ways that gender identities combine with others—such as race, national origin, ethnicity, ability, etc.—and collide with the forces of colonization, class, exploitation-economics, and imperialist capitalism. Trans womanist theology contributes to Trans-Forming Proclamation through emphasis on intersectional power dynamics, the primacy of bodiedness, recognition of a multiplicity of sexualities, and the emphasis on liberative justice for all persons who are women.

That said, a trans-forming methodology also parts ways with traditional forms of ecclesiastical apologetics and permission seeking. Claiming our outcast status as a position of power, centering ourselves and our God-seeking, sanctuary-making processes outside the fabricated walls of buildings, we take our natural place in the primal Grove where Holy Otherness comes seeking us, ever calling us into being and into becoming more authentically who we are. The Sacred Grove is our church, to turn a phrase. There, we write and lift our own hymns and join our voices with the songs of birds, crickets, and katydids. Hummingbird moths, slumbering snakes, and grasshoppers celebrate our calls to worship. We transcend the "church" in all its traditional forms.

What I mean to say is, rather than adapting ourselves to troubling doctrines, compromising our spiritual health, and generally contorting our enspirited bodies to fit into the confining spaces of churches, synagogues, or other houses of prayer, we exist as our authentic selves, adapt and reshape our space, and invite others to meet us there. We engage relational, faith-forming, encounters with scriptures, our sense of God, others, and the world, through our many ways of knowing, intuiting, searching, and discovering, anywhere and everywhere we happen to be, boldly, bravely, and without apology, and invite others who are willing to dare to dream with us. Our authority to do so arises in our being sacred, set-apart people, endowed with Holy Otherness spirit—from our place as Grove-dwelling persons born in the endlessly unfolding divine imaginary.

What Are the Assumptions of Trans-Forming Proclamation?

Foremost of my assumptions are that our primary and most impactful proclamation is expressed by our own gender-transcendent survival, together with our diverse abilities to seek thriving. In other words, our enlivened abilities to persist amid multiple forms of erasure, persecution, marginalization, and oppression are, in and of themselves, living proclamations. This is the "daring existence" I introduced in Chapter 1 and that I have expounded throughout this project.

Through an expansive diversity, this living proclamation peels away layers of assimilated, imposed assumptions to reveal core attributes of human nature. To be a human being is to be endowed with identity—that is, a subjective sense of personhood that somehow pre-exists, yet comes into fullness of being in the relational world. We bear a beingness bodied, simultaneously, in the *now*, the *before*, and the *yet to come*; a selfhood, sensing and asserting an insistent, particular "I am." We experience and manifest a persistent *is-ness* of being, of selfhood, consisting in blood and skin and bone, yet always something *more*, something necessarily bodied and more-than-bodied. To be a person is to be, always, in persistent, particular states of past, present, and future—beingness, becoming-ness, and yet-to-be-ness, endowed with identity, and compelled to manifest, express, and fulfill the selfhood burgeoning within—and to do so in some measure of community with others who are seeking to do the same in the world we inhabit.

The essential attribute of selfhood, as I have discussed, is our disposition toward and capacity for continuous, multilayered states of longing. I have proposed that this disposed capacity is characteristic of what it means to be both human beings and to be spiritual. The liberative implications are powerful. The more that our longing is consumed with meeting the barest survival needs, the more challenging it is to fulfill our deeper longings for actualized personhood, for relational connections, community, sense of purpose, participatory contribution, and, certainly, for thriving. As people who are pressed to the margins of oppressive margins, the more our striving for an authentic sense of self suffers the weights and strains of the world of constructs. And yet, we rise into our own becoming. Selfhood remains. Selfhood survives. In spite of everything that seeks to submerge, subjugate, or destroy the endowed, indwelling sense of selfhood, selfhood rises. Selfhood persists. Selfhood asserts personhood. And personhood proclaims.

This state of being in an unfolding state of endowed selfhood is shared by all of us earth-bound beings. But, the living proclamation of gender-transcendent persons speaks an essential, indisputable truth: the truth of human embodiment is, and always has been, that there are as many ways to be a person—as many gender, sex, sexuality, other possibilities, and unique potentialities—as there are now, ever have been, or ever will be human beings. To be a being of creation is, by nature, to be a distinct, unique expression of embodied *being*. We further proclaim that neither the substance (that is, the essence) nor the value of a human being can be reduced merely to the presence and configuration of hormones, chromosomes, genitals, reproductive organs, primary and secondary sex characteristics; the presumed assignment of these into two, and only two, sexes; or to their supposedly corresponding gender forms, expressions, or self-understandings. No amount of external pressure or imposed regulation can alter the fact that the gloriously persistent sense of who we are will assert selfhood. We inevitably rise up to manifest our truest self, which transcends more limited iterations of us.

As powerful as these truths are, we also testify to an equally inescapable reality. Though the identity with which we are all endowed can never be fully erased, our bodies can be harmed; our psyches can be traumatized; we can be hurt and more than a little broken. Yet, through our very existence in a world that wishes us silent, invisible, or extinct, we proclaim survival. I touched on this wisdom in Chapter 5 as I sorted out what we can learn from Divine Surgery about the powerful gifts our own trans-formations, and our life-ways, offer to the continually unfolding, evolving understanding of what it is to be a human person. The discussion of slipping skin, Chapter 6, speaks most clearly to the wisdom that lies within our deepest knowing. Namely, I posit that our deeply mystical, yet practical abilities to intuit, imagine, and work for our own continual becoming is a life-way disposition necessary to all who long for authentic selfhood—to, in fact, all forms of growth, development, and personal evolution. These knowledge-ways, in fact, enable us to find ways to thrive, flourish, heal, and become the persons only we can be; the persons burgeoning within, longing to be born again, daily, in the ever-evolving process of manifesting the self we are always becoming.

Another defining feature of Trans-Forming Proclamation inheres in the inclination and ability, within many of us, to sense some measure of Sacred Spirit, to discern an engaged and engaging faith, and to locate ourselves within that faith. These yearnings represent profound forms of proclamation. These expressions are sufficiently valid on their own merit. Trans-Forming Proclamation also assumes—and asserts—that all of us, each and every one of us, who long for some measure of connection with this force-presence we call God are fully capable of reading, reflecting upon, and drawing meaning from that body of ancient stories, poems, mythic histories, and faith-filled legends we deem sacred.

In fact, *theology*, in its most basic definition, is simply the *study of God*. More pointedly, I argued in Chapter 3 that our stories of God far exceed what traditional theologies allow. From this perspective, we can be assured that every individual person who searches for some meaningful sense of God or gods or even no-gods actually engages the work of theology. The process of searching for God, thinking about God, reflecting upon the potential nature and actions of God, making interpretations about God, and drawing personal meaning, even perhaps comfort—and sometimes, no comfort—in our searching, are all ways that we "study" God.

No degree or academic education is necessary or required. All of us can—and do—*do theology*. Whether we think of it as theology or not, every time we make statements or assertions about our under-standings or experiences of God, we are making theological procla-mations, which, I might add, are valid in every way because they are ours. So, Trans-Forming Proclamation also opens up an entire are-na, only hinted at in this volume, whereby our Trans-Forming lives are more fully honored for their theological import.

Trans-Forming Proclamation, lifts-up and celebrates all the in-sight-bearing faith-claims revealed in the processes of searching and discerning and recognizes these as valid, important, and spiritually enriching. Said another way: Trans-Forming Proclamations encom-pass all manner of God-seeking, spirit-searching discoveries about God, about ourselves, and about our common lot that emerge in our process—and not only those pursuits that are formally or informal-ly ordained by the church or other religious organizations. In this work, Trans-Forming Proclamation is, and becomes, a trans-forming theology. Even for those of us who are unconcerned with the idea of God, who are not compelled to search for some sense of Sacred Spirit, or even to think about it, our lives are proclamations—to the spirit of life itself, to the vast diversity of everything, to the incom-prehensible current of selfhood-vitality innately present in all that is.

That is, as gender-transcendent persons our lives are shaped, formed, and informed by our trans-formed experiences, perspectives, encounters, knowledge-ways, and wisdoms, and our lives speak to the vitality and insistence of life engaged in becoming and living on. And, for those of us who search for some sense of God and of who God is in our lives, who discern experiences of relationship with God, our lives speak pronouncements of continually trans-formed experiences, insights, revelations, and wisdom. We and our search-ing for and our discovering of God are always emerging in an on-going process of formation. Our *study of God*—our "theology"—is trans-shaped, trans-formed, and trans-informed. Therefore, it arises through, pertains to, and offers meaning within the whole of our psychodynamic, social, and spiritual needs, experiences, and ways of being. Our work and our proclaiming, then, need not be about *only* gender, sex, sexuality, or about taking apart the specific verses employed against us—though there is, always, rich ground there, still to be excavated.

Finally, Trans-Forming Proclamation assumes that our very lives—even, and perhaps, especially, *our bodies*—are also sacred texts of a kind. Our embodied selves are sacred. We are holy, living, speaking, and testifying, embodied texts of survival *trans-formed* into persistent, insistent living-on. We are miracles of an ever-evolving, endlessly creating, Life-Source Imaginer of persons. The lessons born within us, through our blood and bones and our stories, are holy, set-apart lessons. The stories we carry in spirit-skin—enfleshed-essence—are body-etched and life-uttered scriptures of a particular kind. Our existence is a living testament to the many ways God comes to us and makes revelations, everywhere. In varying degrees, these things are true of all human beings—of creation, entirely—but they are true of us in unique, sacredness-expanding ways that reveal needful bits and pieces of insights for deeper understanding, not only of who God might be, but also of who we human creatures are and might be.

Moreover, in Chapter 7, especially, I proposed that—as gender-transcendent persons—in our *otherness*, our sanctified *set-apartness*, and our threshold-crossing capacities, we are much nearer to the wholly Holy Other than we have been led to believe by God-hoarding, and manipulating, aristocracy who fear us and wish us extinct. This reality offers us a powerful point of engagement with the texts we have been given, as well as with the texts of history, world, culture, society, and especially, faith traditions. It positions us in the rich Grove-ground of becoming, where all that is, was, or ever will be originates and emboldens us to take our particular, set-apart place as diverse, individuated children of the Great Imaginer.

In our struggles and our thriving, in our staying-in and our going-out, in our seemingly stalling self-doubt and our working-it-all-out, in our hurt and our healing, in our sorrow and our joy, in our fear and our bravery, we speak—often, without ever uttering a self-revealing word. Through our many particular ways of being, persisting, and resisting extinction, we speak to the diversity of ways that

Source of everything is present and manifesting everywhere, moves in human conditions and affairs, self-discloses through embodied living stories, and, thus, perhaps transforms not only us, especially, but all of us earth-bound beings.

Trans-Forming Proclamation remembers, lifts up, and honors the sanctuary Grove as the place where outcast peoples gather together, build, and strengthen community. We engage communally with some sense of Holy Presence and, in so doing, make proclamations. The Grove is recognizable as a powerful allegory for the *other*-space to which we, especially—as persons living outside accepted regulations of gender, sex, and sexuality—are drawn, longing, discerning something more within ourselves, and daring to express it. Equally, the Grove is a vibrant, useful illustrative model for the kind of proclamation I am describing in this book.

All that we proclaim, as gender-diverse and gender-expansive persons, is *Grove-proclamation* of a kind. It is the bold, unapologetic, and intentional act of professing the realities of Grove-spaces nestled and nurtured within our outcast communities, disdained and forgotten, expected to keep silent and unseen. Such proclamation breaks silences and moves outcast revelations from the hiddenness of the Grove outward into the world of others. In so doing, the truth-claims we make, everywhere, are Grove-born proclamations: from the living facts of our survival to the affirmations we voice in speeches, songs, and shouts; the realities we articulate in chants raised at marches and rallies, small and large; the awarenesses we raise at forums, teach-ins, cafes, coffee shops, and street corners. Everywhere and every way, we raise the cry for freedom to be and become more fully ourselves is a place of Grove-inspired, Trans-Forming Proclamation.

And, equally, the bold witness of words set forth in speeches, papers, books, poems, songs, and messages delivered from pulpits, lecterns, podiums, and stages are also profound Grove-enlivened proclamations. When we speak in classrooms, town halls, vigils, and other courageous conversations, we proclaim. When we dare to profess and affirm our shared humanity, we are proclaiming. When we assert our inherent rights to dignified, flourishing selfhood and assurance of place in community, we embody this proclamation. When we assert that these inherent dignities are espoused and confirmed in all our religions, our imaginings of just coexistence, and all our dreams of freedom, we make proclamations.

Practicing Trans-Forming Proclamation

Carrying these assumptions and taking our place within the living Grove of gender-transcendent beingness, searching for glimpses of holy-revelation and declaring what comes to us in the process is the work of Trans-Forming Proclamation. In doing this, we enact resistance; we break free from the negations and restrictions placed upon us by the religion-hoarding, God-perverting, exclusionary tradition-keepers. We claim the original promise given to all human beings: to be God's people, to search for God and be accepted by God, and to seek spiritual meaning in body, in world, and in scripture. We make our proclamation our own when we find God in the texts of life and embodied experience, in all forms of sacred words uttered and written across time, cultures, and places. The permission for such searching and proclaiming is *already* given to us by the God who comes, ever-seeking, often in the breezy time of the day, claiming each of us, from Eden to this day and this place.

Knowing this is our right, from Eden to this moment and beyond, perhaps we can feel the Grove calling us to lean into awareness of ourselves and our surroundings, to sense the pulsing of life within and all around us, the kin among us, and to reposition the marvelous facts of ourselves into the bare and essential facts of all the living. There, re-centered within the liminal, vibrant, and vital threshold-space in which we were born, perhaps we can feel ourselves compelled to speak: to shout, whisper, and perhaps to sing; to write, dance, draw, or sculpt; ultimately, to live on: to make and create space to live an authentic, audacious proclamation.

With a hope of avoiding oversimplification, it seems helpful to reiterate core points proposed in this project in ways that describe and affirm practices lifted-up as trans-formed, and trans-forming, ways of thinking, reflecting, interpreting, and making truth-bearing claims. From the context of the positions proposed in this work, I am proposing the following working summarial list:

≈ **Returning to the Grove:** claiming our place as miraculous beings born into and recalling (proclaiming) a magical, par-ticularity-infused divine imaginary of beings; boldly living on: in whatever ways are authentic and meaningful for us, to make our lives worth living, and assist us in achieving some measures of thriving, safety, belonging, and purpose, our liv-ing on is essential and a profound proclamation; and daring existence in ways that seek and discover relational connec-tions in a world that wishes us invisible and works for our erasure.

≈ **Crossing over, again and again:** claiming our thresh-old-crossing skills and gifts; defiant, embodied, mystical/intuitive transit through the world of constructs that hon-ors the sacred reality of natural boundaries and reveals bi-naries-rejecting realities of false margins; claiming and ex-ercising our threshold-crossing, margin-revealing powers to develop and nurture pragmatic, relational/communal inter-dependence and sanctuary spaces.

≈ **Emerging and re-emerging from the Grove:** employing the world-changing mystical power in the matter of words, *and of bodies,* of conjuring through story, naming, re-nam-ing, re-dressing, and re-shaping language, bodies, spaces, and world.

≈ **Shedding skins:** not only of ill-fitting gender and sex as-sumptions, but also of the harmful mythologies of white supremacy, misogynistic androcentrism, class, ableism, etc., revealing through the power of presence the truth that there are as many bodied, wise, and wonderful ways to be a human being as there are now, ever have been, or ever will be human persons.

≈ **Conjuring a sensibility, a lived methodology:** transcending binary divisions through personal presence and relationship—including, the power of learning to filter through our own experience for the purpose of filtering-in the experience of others not like ourselves, finding common power and shared wisdom through differences and distinctions.

≈ **Reading self, world, others, scripture, nature, history, and experience trans-marginally:** drawing on the knowledge-ways, life-ways, and experiences of our own positions to learn to recognize, acknowledge the experiences, knowledge, and wisdom of others not like ourselves that make us able to continuing shedding ill-suited skins—remembering, we do not need to disclose our gender-transcendent identities to speak from the wisdom of our experiences and connect with others.

≈ **A method in which we dare to be broken open:** to be like construct-defying living, breathing, bodied geode-beings, breaking open ourselves in ways that break open the truth-obscuring gunk covering the larger geode-world, laying bare death-dealing binaries, imposed absolutes, constructed ideas, practices that prevent flourishing.

≈ **Seeking to think, reflect, and engage in ways that affirm a Womanist perspective:** a pragmatic approach that does not leave behind the poor or nonwhite, that does not just focus on equality with men, that uses intersectional power analysis as a vantage point to visions of greater equity and solutions-seeking.

≈ **Transgressing and trans-forming marginalizing barriers:** by turning our ways of knowing, imagining, and conjuring liberating wisdoms and life-ways toward dismantling colonization and white supremacy, deconstructing systems of privileging, restoring natural boundaries of personhood, land, and other beings in all our work for change.

≈ **Trans-forming theologies—including queer theories— we have been given:** by reading trans-marginally; reading texts of bodies, experiences, history, world, and scripture beyond traditional visioning, interpreting and reflecting through our gender-transcendent ways of knowing, thinking, being, and doing the living of our lives.

≈ **Daring to claim the contribution of our lives:** to the ongoing, still-being-written, ever-unfolding story of humanity without seeking approval, or validation, and most surely without asking permission to express the insights, wisdom, and knowledge we discern from our own powerful, magical, threshold-crossing, miraculous lives.

≈ **Daring to live, speak, and proclaim our gifts:** of our truth-claims, our relational testimonies, and spiritual wisdoms born in personal experiences of this Force-Presence we call God—and most especially, to testify to and proclaim the discernments and wisdoms we discover as mystical, marvelous beings of the Sacred Grove seeking bodied sovereignty and sanctuary in the worlds we inhabit.

To summarize, Trans-Forming Proclamation is an expression of diverse gender-transcendent embodiments daring to live on; it is a necessary and life-affirming way of thinking and of proposing truths and faith-claims about gender-transcendent beingness, God, and spiritual experiences in a precarious world. It assumes our origins and positions in a gender and sex threshold-crossing holy *other-space*. People of the persisting primeval Grove, in testament to the vibrant particularity of life, we exist; we persist; and we strive for ways to thrive, to make for ourselves lives imbued with meaning—lives worth living.

Carrying the Sacred Grove with us, we *remember* the Grove by locating and creating spaces of shelter, support, and sustenance. This, we must do because we are Grove-born beings living in a world of others confounded by our presence; we live and move in an ill-fitting world, ill-prepared for us. Therefore, we are moving, always, back and forth, crossing over thresholds between spaces befitting to us and spaces inhospitable; spaces of shelter and some measure of security and spaces hostile to us. We are borderland people, beings of the Sacred Grove, where the Maker of holy imaginaries abides with us, celebrating our embodied lives, always crossing over and between the sacred everywhere-spaces we inhabit to the spaces and places we must learn to navigate in the day-to-day world of human constructs.

As such, gender-transcendent persons offer vital insights, testimonies, and miraculous stories to the larger, ongoing human search for apprehending some sense of who God is and who we are in relation to this *Holy Otherness* and to each other. Trans-formed proclamations attest to the reality that we can be hurt, abused, traumatized, and a little broken in our earth-walking, but we can never be fully controlled, subjugated, silenced, or erased. This reality, itself, is an ongoing, living proclamation.

We testify that neither the essence nor worth of a person can be reduced to imposed binary codifications of gender, sex, and/or sexuality, especially, nor to other embodied factors such as race, ethnicity, or ability. Precisely because ideologies and systems exist that aim toward confining and erasing us, we are uniquely formed, positioned, and equipped to make particularly significant declarations about life, lived conditions, faith, and justice. Locating our living proclamation within images of the Grove speaks not only to resisting extinction, both ours and our planet's, but also to all that is revealed in the resilience of living on—of bearing forth embodied is-ness, of manifesting the germinal ground of beingness originations and potentialities.

This is not a reactionary process. It is a continuing, developing process of being. Living on in search of authentic selfhood, like branches reaching toward the sun, speaks the ever-evolving, diversely individuated, yet shared, living language of becoming. We are neither for nor against the church. We are beyond it.

What I mean to say, as clearly as possible, is this: rooting our living proclamations in the image of the primal Grove reclaims the inherent, adaptively intentional, and biologically necessary diversity of all life—including, us, most surely. All human beings, and therefore, gender-transcendent persons, belong to a vast, ever-emerging and evolving, complex, needfully interconnected web of biological diversity. At every material and elemental level, we exist. Simply, and profoundly, we are. We are, equally, beyond the constructed world.

Trans-beingness is not a reaction to narrowly defined, controlling, and divisive gender reductionism. Systems of gender reductivity *are a reaction to us.* Just as the Grove simply is—just as it exists in a web of diverse, interconnected, interdependent arising—we simply are. And, just as the marvelously inter-webbed, yet individuated elements, matter, living beings and things within it are essential to the Grove, we are needful to the whole of a relationally connected, interdependent, flourishing humanity. We are. We exist. And we are as essential to the whole of creation as hummingbird moths, duck-billed platypuses, hawthorn trees, cisgender women, and cisgender men. We are and our simply being testifies to the bold bareness of life, entire and ever-evolving.

Further, as bold, enduring expressions of the persistent, bare insistence of life, we claim the same original promise of all human beings: that the Many-Named Holy Otherness is our God and we are people of Holy Otherness. As such, our faith-claims as gender-transcendent persons are as valid, pertinent, and informative to a larger process of discerning God and faith as any other—perhaps, given our threatened existence, more so than other dominant narratives.

Asserting these propositions, and the hopes borne within them, is ultimately the substance of this book: a written reflection, returning to the endlessly, existence-proclaiming cosmic Sacred Grove; it is to take a position in that *other*-space, to testify to it, and to proclaim all that we discern and receive in that place.

Epilogue: Unmistakable Sounds

Here, on the screened porch: dusk descends,
moving evening toward morning, again, a succession
of days. In a relative stillness, and just moments ago,

I heard the unmistakable sounds of music, and singing—
birdsong whistles and calls; cascading cricket string-legs
humming, bowed beneath resonator-wings; leaves and whisper-thin
branches, rustling and flapping, stirred by rising breezes—
I am almost sure it was God's voice cantoring, gathering
all the living in bursts of boundless proclamation.

Though I am not certain, I sense I know the tune; familiar,
it just may be the same tender song my own soul sings in quietude—
perhaps, hearing it, more and again, I will know it surely.

For now, rain too is coming, descending—big,
randomly pelting drops greet the ground with tiny splashes;
making way, preparing for the swelling quenching—doubtless,
a cleansing. Still now, a distant dove mourns discernable sounds
of spirit lifting; rising on prayers too full for words: the remains
of mystery, meeting my own softer murmuring drones.

Though one can never be too certain, I am almost sure: this—
these unmistakable arrangements—this too, is God's voice
meeting us, together, across the expanse, beyond the distances,
unfolding, singing things far too full for words, emerging over
and over, and surely, delighting.

resources
for the journey

While the ideas and analyses in this work are my own, nothing comes to be in a vacuum. And, though it is impossible to list all the authors and books that have influenced my formation, I do want to offer some suggestions for further reading that I believe are a good sampling of my own reading and inquiries. These include some older works that I return to, sometimes wrestle with, and always benefit from reengaging. Additionally, I have listed some newer works. This list is, by no means, exhaustive or representative of the eclectic range of things I read, but in various ways, they relate to the topics in this work.

Armstrong, Karen. *A History of God: The 4,000-Year Quest of Judaism, Christianity, and Islam*, Ballantine Books, New York, 1993.

Byrd, Jodi A. *The Transit of Empire: Indigenous Critiques of Colonialism.* University of Minnesota Press, Minneapolis, 2011.

Copeland, M. Shawn. *Enfleshing Freedom: Body, Race, and Being.* Fortress Press, Minneapolis, 2010.

Davis, Angela Y. *Freedom Is a Constant Struggle: Ferguson, Palestine, and the Foundations of a Movement.* Haymarket Books, Chicago, 2016.

Drinkwater, Gregg, Joshua Lesser, David Shneer, editors. *Torah Queeries: Weekly Commentaries on the Hebrew Bible.* New York University Press, New York, 2009.

Edwards, Denis. *How God Acts: Creation, Redemption, and Special Divine Action*. Fortress Press, Minneapolis, 2010.

Eagleton, Terry. *Why Marx Was Right*. Yale University Press, New Haven and London, 2011.

Grant, Jacquelyn. *White Women's Christ and Black Women's Jesus: Feminist Christology and Womanist Response*. Scholars Press, Atlanta, 1989.

hooks, bell. *Outlaw Culture: Resisting Representations*. Routledge Classics, New York, 1994, 2006.

Isenberg, Nancy. *White Trash: The 400-Year Untold History of Class in America*. Penguin Books, New York, 2016.

Jung, Carl G. *The Undiscovered Self.* Atlantic Monthly Press, Little, Brown, and Company, Boston, Toronto, 1957, Second Printing.

Kaldera, Raven. *Hermaphrodeities: The Transgender Spirituality Workbook, 2nd Edition*. Asphodel Press, Hubbardston, MA, 2008.

Lorde, Audre. *Sister Outsider: Essays and Speeches*. Crossing Press Feminist Series, Berkeley, 1984.

MacLean, Nancy. *Democracy in Chains: The Deep History of the Radical Right's Plan for America*. Scribe Publications, London, 2017.

Moraga, Cherrie and Gloria Anzaldua, editors. *This Bridge Called My Back: Writings by Radical Women of Color, Fourth Edition*. State University of New York, Albany, 2015. (Earlier editions, which I first read, are out of print.)

Rogers, Carl. *On Becoming a Person: A Therapist's View of Psychotherapy*. Houghton Mifflin Co., Boston, New York, 1961, 1995.

Williams, Delores S. *Sisters in the Wilderness: The Challenge of Womanist God-Talk.* Orbis Books, Maryknoll, 1993.

BIBLE STUDY AIDS:

The Blue Letter Bible: This tool is a good standard for both the Hebrew texts and the Greek (Christian) texts. Here is the link: www.blueletterbible.org.

BibleWebApp: This tool is more useful for people who have some knowledge of the Hebrew and Greek texts, but it can function as a general point of reference for getting a basic sense of the text. I use "Version 1" when I need a quick prompt or refresher because I like the format better. Here is the link: biblewebapp.com.

Brown-Driver-Briggs Hebrew and English Lexicon, Francis Brown, S. R. Driver, Charles Briggs, editors; Snowball Publishing, 2010 (original 1906).
This is the primary lexicon for serious students of Hebrew. However, I do not recommend trying to teach oneself Hebrew, but it is a necessary resource for students of Hebrew and certainly good for people with Hebrew-reading friends who can help.

Index to *Brown-Driver-Briggs Hebrew and English Lexicon,* compiled by Bruce Einspahr; Moody Publishers, Chicago, 1976. This index is a huge time-saving addition to deep study of Hebrew. Without it, one has to know one's Hebrew rather well to avoid getting lost in the BDB Lexicon.

***The Jewish Annotated New Testament,* Second Edition, New Revised Standard Version,** Amy-Jill Levine and Marc Zvi Brettler, editors; Oxford University Press, New York, 2011, 2017.
This offering of scholarly Jewish perspectives is essential to a more

informed understanding of Jesus and the development of ideas and perspectives known to us as Christianity. This book is a must-have for people who wish to broaden their range of interpretation.

The Jewish Study Bible featuring the Jewish Publication Society Tanakh Translation, Adele Berlin and Marc Zvi Brettler, editors; Oxford University Press, New York, 2004.
Although the JPS translation is not always as good as it could be, the commentaries, essays, maps, and other educational material are excellent resources. This text is a must-have for people who are serious about developing a more Jewish-respecting understanding of the Hebrew scriptures, as well as historical and cultural contexts.

Tanach: The Torah, Prophets, Writings: The Twenty-four-Books of the Bible Newly Translated and Annotated, The Stone Edition Artscroll Series, Rabbi Nossom Scherman, editor; Mesorah Publications, Ltd, Brooklyn, 1996.
This particular edition of the Hebrew Bible is, by far, one of the best. The commentaries, essays, and references to rabbinical interpretation are impeccable.

TRANS-SPECIFIC RESOURCES:

OtherWise Christian: A Guidebook for Transgender Liberation, Mx Chris Paige, author; OtherWise Engaged Publishing, 2019.
This is the definitive compilation, analysis, and commentary on trans-liberating theology. This book also provides an excellent working bibliography of the foundational works in trans theology. Therefore, I am not adding my own rather broad, diverse, ever-growing reading list.

OtherWise Christian 2: Stories of Resistance, Mx Chris Paige, editor; OtherWise Engaged Publishing, 2020.

acknowledgments

Accepting the clichés, it is still true that the project of a book never comes into being without the accompaniment, help, and work of others. First and foremost, and with some measure of emotion, I want to express my deep, layered gratitude to my editor, Mx Chris Paige, without whom this project likely never would have launched, let alone been completed. Chris and I have long been peers, colleagues, collaborators, and, most especially, friends. However, engaging this work together has deepened and expanded our relationship in ways I could never have imagined and for which I am profoundly grateful. The gift of friendship—of being seen, known, accepted, challenged, encouraged, held carefully accountable for growth, and loved—far exceeds the gift of these pages. I have discovered, in our relationship, a kinship and unconditional accompaniment that have changed me in ways I am still processing. I cannot speak for my friend, but I think we are both better for this journey. I know I am. I am a more clear and careful thinker, a better writer, and more—a better self for our long trek through these pages.

Chris: you are not only brilliant in a multitude of ways, you are also a gifted and insightful reader-editor, coach, cheerleader, compassionate challenger, and mindful creative partner. More than this, your gifts are extraordinary: for sensing the hidden, stifled voice within, for discerning long-built barriers to a self longing to speak, and for holding friendship in the most caring and healing of ways—even as a self breaks open in your company. I cannot think of anyone I would want to do this work with, and my gratitude surpasses my meager gifts with words.

Revolutions are cumulative. Thus, a synergism of creative, supportive, encouraging, and equally challenging forces built this book. I began forming the bones of this work more than four years ago. Much of the content appeared in various forms, over time, through workshops, blog posts, sermons, speeches, and other writing. I began working on various drafts, before Chris and I began the actual production of the book in 2019. Around that time, due to nonprofit funding challenges, I had to attempt returning to mainstream employment. All the while, I was writing—at night, on the weekends, sometimes in the middle of the night.

Along the way, I suffered some experiences on the job that reactivated old traumas and caused some new ones. I struggled. Through all of this, my spouse and my family hung in there and continued to love and support me—even when I was not so easy to love. Chris, too, hung in there with me, as did my therapist. Ultimately, the book, as it is now, was formed in the midst of all of that recovery, self-searching, healing, and movement forward. The power of this process, along with my spouse, my family, Chris, and my friends, saved me.

In this very public space, I will simply say this to Diana, my spouse: I am grateful, every single day, that I have lived on and that we, older and wiser and more settled, found each other again. Second chances come to few of us. I am a better, more loving, and more engaged person because of us, because we got a second chance. I love you, and I know this book contains more than your wise proofreading, creative design, and compositing genius. It contains your love as much as it contains some measure of my own.

My rabbi, Mark Cohn, with whom I share *Chavruta*, is, indeed, my *yedid chaver*, my beloved friend—long before he became my rabbi. Our rich study and Mark's wisdom, knowledge of Talmud, Jewish history, humor, and deep spirituality are constant companions. Much gratitude to my Hebrew professor, Clinton Moyer, Ph.D., who (thank God for graduation!) is also my friend and interpretive thought-partner. Learning to recognize the literary depth of Jewish texts, including non-canonical texts, the gift of merisms and other tropes, and my growing love of Hebrew, itself, are gifts from Clinton. I am also grateful to, and for, Naomi Greenberg and Rabbi Joshua Lesser.

I am grateful for and acknowledge the constancy of my mother, my father, and my stepmother. Our son, Lucas, has borne witness, gifted me with patience, and believed in me in ways that sustain me beyond measure. My family has been equally patient and supportive.

I keep on keeping on, in large part, because I am loved—and al-

acknowledgments

lowed to love—a host of people who also just happen to be Bible geeks, faith partners, thought-companions, and co-conspirators in dreaming a better world. This list is not comprehensive, by far, but holds the gathering of witnesses to, and sojourners with, this particular project; gratitude and so much love to: Peterson Thomas Toscano, partner in the revolution; Louis Mitchell, beloved friend and trusted companion; Karon and Jason McKinney, thank you for the music—many days, your voices carried me through.

There are several people who also graciously agreed to read and review this work. Kate Bornstein, for loving and believing so hard and long enough, that I began to believe in myself; my gratitude is deep. I've loved you long and I love you still. Rabbi Mark Sameth: for rich, long-distance chavruta, insightful teaching, and especially, for solidarity with our gender-transcendent and queer relations, my gratitude remains. I am also grateful for, and uplifted by, your kind and generous support of my work. Reverend Donovan Ackley III: I am profoundly grateful for your supportive review of this book and affirmed by your praise and enthusiasm. I very much look forward to what emerges between us as we travel along. Diamond Stylz: thank you so much, dear sibling, for your accompaniment, your generosity of spirit and time, and your heartfelt support of me, the book, and the Bible Bash. More, thank you for the gift of your deep laughter, especially amid the tears, and for shared heart through the years along our connected journeys. Enzi Tanner: there is so much to say, chaver. For now, I will simply say thank you for being who you are in my life and in our shared communities; I am better for your wise and loving company. Mycroft Masada: nu, in addition to my appreciation for your insights, questions, and clever wit, it is my great joy to be held in our friendship every time I wear the tallit. To both of you, Enzi and Mycroft: immeasurable gratitude for riding together in the chariot!

Lastly, I am grateful beyond measure to those people who, all along, accompanied me in learning to believe in living-on and doing the work of saving my own ass. Many thanks to Joy Ladin for journeying companionship—and for the company of your poetry.

So much gratitude to Andy Moretz (too much to say here). Many thanks to all my recovering companions far and wide. Love and gratitude to the Rev. Willard Bass; the Rev. Don Durham; and Meredith Doster, Ph.D. Deep, abiding love and appreciation for my close friends and colleagues: the Rev. Dawn Flynn; the Rev. Debra Hopkins; Pastor Mykal Shannon; and, especially, to all my gender-transcendent kindred, far and wide, who have mentored and accompanied me, allowed me to mentor and accompany you, and who, in your living-on, give me hope, strength, and a sense of Holy Otherness passing by—so much of this work is for you.

in remembrance

During the final production stages of this book, our communities were shaken by the loss of two beloved kindred—both gender-transcendent elders, mentors, friends, colleagues, and tireless advocates, change-makers, boat-rockers, and visionaries whose lives impacted so many of us, in ways too large to fully describe. Their passing not only touched me and my life in significant ways, but also touched our communities and all those involved in the production of this book in personal and distinct ways. I cannot close this work without offering remembrance.

Monica Roberts—Moni to friends and various relations—founder of TransGriot, history-keeper, storyteller, and tireless trans advocate, passed October 5, 2020. In honoring my sense of Monica and my deep regard, respect, and love for her, I will share a story that describes the enduring image I carry of her. We met in a trans-typical way, at a trans conference in Charlotte, North Carolina, in 2011. After engaging with one another in a workshop, she hugged me and proclaimed a hearty "welcome home." We shared hugs every time we were together. And every time, from the first hug to the last, I was struck by how stately and majestic, yet warm, kind, and accessible she was. After all, Monica was tall and, in our communities, she was (and is still) larger than life. But the really meaningful, beautiful thing is that, despite my small stature—it always felt like my head fell somewhere between her waist and her ribcage—I never felt small next to Moni. In fact, something about being seen, embraced, and loved by Monica always made me feel strangely taller, uplifted, and like I could be and do more than imagined. I share this because, to my heart-mind, that is who Monica was. She made us all feel seen, welcomed, loved, and a little bit bigger and braver than we ever thought.

I would be lying if I tried to say that something of that same uplifting way of being does not lie at the core of my dreams for this book. I can only hope to achieve, in my own way with this book, some small measure of the same affirming inspiration Monica lived in our world. Monica: I will ever carry you with me.

Virginia Ramey Mollenkott, PhD, also passed on during the final stages of producing this book. In many ways, this book is a kind of full-circle honoring of my connections to Virginia. In 1978, Virginia and Letha Dawson Scanzoni published a book that was the very first of its kind: a call to Christians to reassess and examine their condemnation of lesbian, gay, and bisexual persons, titled *Is the Homosexual My Neighbor: A Positive Christian Response.* At the time, I was in high school, coming out in all sorts of ways, and struggling. The pastor at our Baptist church (yes, a Baptist pastor) had been working with me around the whole God and religion mess. He took me to meet Letha and she gifted me a hardback copy of the book, right out of the box-full in her office. The book, their words and insights, saved me. Literally.

For years thereafter, I read everything Virginia wrote that I could get my hands on. Later, *Omnigender: A Trans-religious Approach,* was there to help me through reckoning with the gender I had so long suppressed. Social media made it possible to connect with Virginia in more personal ways. During the production of this book, through their very personal relationship, Chris provided Virginia with a reader's copy of the manuscript. Graciously and in ways expressive of who Virginia was, the good Doctor was anxious to read it. We were mindful of the illness Virginia was suffering. Chris and I, both, hoped and prayed for Virginia's recovery. Sadly, Virginia passed on September 25, 2020. For me, however, the gift of Virginia's willingness to read my little offering and celebrate it with me (with us) is one of the most meaningful things I have ever received. It is a kind of homecoming.

Even as it is, ultimately, for all of us, this book is dedicated to Monica and Virginia. Zikronam livracha: may their memories be for a blessing...and may that blessing be ongoing revelation and revolution.

about the author

Liam Michael Hooper (liammichaelhooper.com) is a theological activist and transgender advocate with a Master of Divinity degree from Wake Forest University. Formerly ordained clergy in the United Church of Christ, Hooper has recently converted to Judaism.

For over thirty years, Hooper has advocated for safe, person-centered, affirming healthcare for LGBTQIA individuals. He has served in counseling, case management, and clinical director roles, serving community members struggling with HIV or addictions. He has also volunteered with a variety of LGBTQIA-centered organizations. He is especially passionate about facilitating interfaith and intra-agency collaboration.

Liam is the founder of a North Carolina nonprofit called Ministries Beyond Welcome (ministriesbeyondwelcome.org), which celebrates the inherent worth, vitality, and indomitable spirit of gender-transcendent communities through education, organizing, collaboration, and support. As part of that work, he co-hosts The Bible Bash podcast with Peterson Toscano.

Liam has been named to the 2020–2022 cohort of The William C. Friday Fellowship for Human Relations, a prestigious non-partisan leadership program in North Carolina. His writing has been featured in the OtherWise Christian series, and he has worked extensively with the Transfaith community.

He lives in North Carolina with his spouse, Diana, where they raise their son Lucas and their dog Dodi, and are surrounded by family, close friends, and a vibrant Jewish community.

Resources from
OtherWise Engaged Publishing

OtherWise Christian: A Guidebook for Transgender Liberation
by Mx Chris Paige

OtherWise Christian 2: Stories of Resistance
edited by Mx Chris Paige

Christian Faith and Gender Identity:
An OtherWise Reflection Guide
by Mx Chris Paige

In Remembrance of Me, Bearing Witness to Transgender Tragedy:
An OtherWise Reflection Guide
by Mx Chris Paige

From Christendom to Freedom:
Journey-Making with a Black Transgender Elder
by Jonathon Thunderword

And more to come!

Please visits http://otherwiseengaged4u.wordpress.com
to learn more.

OtherWise Engaged Publishing

OtherWise Engaged Publishing is excited to be working with the best and brightest of OtherWise-gendered folk! We provide a multi-tradition, independent publishing operation for projects from OtherWise-gendered folk that are in alignment with our values.

Visit otherwiseengaged4u.wordpress.com
for information about our latest releases
and to support independent transgender-led publishing.

What are the words you do not yet have?
What do you need to say?
What are the tyrannies you swallow day by day
and attempt to make your own,
until you sicken and die of them, still in silence.

~Audre Lorde.

CPSIA information can be obtained
at www.ICGtesting.com
Printed in the USA
LVHW010353050821
694541LV00011B/972

9 781951 124236